VANITY FAIR
PORTRAITS
PHOTOGRAPHS
1913-2008

VANITY FAIR PORTRAITS

PHOTOGRAPHS 1913-2008

DAVID FRIEND
CHRISTOPHER HITCHENS
TERENCE PEPPER

NATIONAL PORTRAIT GALLERY, LONDON

Published in Great Britain by
National Portrait Gallery Publications,
National Portrait Gallery,
St Martin's Place,
London WC2H 0HE

By arrangement with *Vanity Fair*
To accompany the exhibition *Vanity Fair
Portraits: Photographs 1913–2008*
at the National Portrait Gallery, London
14 February–26 May 2008, the Scottish
National Portrait Gallery, Edinburgh
14 June–21 September 2008,
Los Angeles County Museum of Art
26 October 2008–1 March 2009 and
the National Portrait Gallery, Canberra
12 June to 30 August 2009.

For a complete catalogue of current
publications, please write to the
National Portrait Gallery at the address
above, or visit our website at
www.npg.org.uk/publications

ISBN 978 185514 391 3

A catalogue record for this book is
available from the British Library.

For the National Portrait Gallery
Publishing Manager: Celia Joicey
Project Editor: Denny Hemming
Assistant Editor: Claudia Bloch
Production: Ruth Müller-Wirth
Design: Andrew Ross

For *Vanity Fair*
Editors: Graydon Carter and David Friend
Photo Research: Betsy Horan
Art Production: Mimi Park
Production: Martha Hurley
Photo Assistant: Dana Kravis
Editorial Associate: Jessica Flint
Condé Nast Archive: Gretchen Fenston,
Leigh Montville, Shawn Waldron

Typeset in Vanity Fair Sans

Printed in Italy

Editorial Note
Figure captions refer to publication
dates in *Vanity Fair* magazine.
Plate captions refer to the year in
which photographs were actually
taken. Picture Credits give both dates
for reference.

Exhibition sponsored by

BURBERRY
ESTABLISHED 1856

The National Portrait Gallery's
Spring Season 2008 is sponsored
by Herbert Smith LLP

CONTENTS

FOREWORD
SANDY NAIRNE

The phrase 'Vanity Fair', with its origin in John Bunyan's *Pilgrim's Progress*, has a resonance that crosses several centuries. And what is held in common between William Makepeace Thackeray's novel, serialized in *Punch* in 1847, and the British and American periodicals of the same name, published in the later nineteenth century, is their witty, satirical commentary on the culture and society of their time. Condé Nast re-created the international magazine we know today in New York in 1913 – a new incarnation for a new century. It positioned fashion and society alongside current debates within literature and the arts and translated the portrayal of outstanding individuals from drawing or caricature into the most appropriate medium for the modern age – photography.

What the editor Frank Crowninshield, and subsequently Tina Brown and Graydon Carter, knew was that a great portrait photograph could encapsulate much more than the person portrayed. Individuals in the public eye are perceived not only in terms of their achievements but also their connections with those around them, and with a particular moment in time. We chart history through people, and the images that delineate our chronology today are often magazine shots taken by great

photographers from Baron De Meyer, Edward Steichen and Cecil Beaton to Bruce Weber and Annie Leibovitz.

Vanity Fair Portraits came about through the suggestion of Graydon Carter and David Friend, and I am enormously grateful to them for the collaboration that this project – both exhibition and catalogue – represents. By tracing the birth and evolution of photographic portraiture in the twentieth century through 150 of the magazine's most memorable portrait photographs, *Vanity Fair Portraits* affirms a synergy between gallery, magazine and portrait photograph.

Like *Vanity Fair*, the National Portrait Gallery has championed the genre of the portrait photograph. The Gallery's pioneering work began in the 1960s, initiated by its director Sir Roy Strong. The first photographic exhibition held at the Gallery was *Beaton Portraits 1928–1968* in 1968. The two key objectives were to acknowledge the importance of photography and to allow portraits of living celebrities to adorn its walls. Forty years on, the continuing interest in photography requires no further elaboration. Under Colin Ford, the first Keeper of Film and Photography at the Gallery, and now Terence Pepper, the Gallery's commitment has both increased and flourished. It has

focused on creating exhibitions of the work of outstanding individual photographers: Arnold Newman; Norman Parkinson; Bill Brandt; Karsh; Alice Springs and Helmut Newton; Robert Mapplethorpe; Annie Leibovitz; Richard Avedon; James Abbe; Bruce Weber; August Sander; Henri Cartier-Bresson; Snowdon; Horst P. Horst; Philippe Halsman; Mario Testino; Julia Margaret Cameron; and Lee Miller. The Gallery has also made exhibitions that have explored the changing role of photographic portraits, such as *We are the People* in 2004 and *Face of Fashion* in 2007. *Vanity Fair Portraits* embraces both these elements and the work of many of these same photographers has been celebrated equally in the pages of *Vanity Fair* and on the Gallery walls.

We are delighted that, after its London showing, *Vanity Fair Portraits* will be seen at the Scottish National Portrait Gallery, Edinburgh, the Los Angeles County Museum of Art and the National Portrait Gallery, Canberra. I am grateful to James Holloway and Nicola Kalinsky, Michael Govan, and Irene Martin and Andrew Sayers for working with us to make this possible.

Fuller acknowledgements are given elsewhere, but my very considerable thanks go to Terence Pepper and David Friend as the

joint curators of the exhibition. Their detailed researches on the *Vanity Fair* story are a substantial achievement at the heart of the project. I should like to thank Christopher Hitchens for his brilliant commentary on the idea of *Vanity Fair*. My sincere thanks also go to Claire Everitt and Rosie Wilson as Exhibitions Managers, Celia Joicey as Publications Manager, Sarah Tinsley as Head of Exhibitions, Pim Baxter as Communications and Development Director, Jude Simmons as Head of Design and Naomi Conway as Head of Corporate Development. Chris Garrett, Edward Menicheschi and Sara Marks, and many colleagues at *Vanity Fair* and the Condé Nast Archive have all made outstanding efforts to bring this project to fruition.

I should also like to offer my special thanks to Christopher Bailey, Angela Ahrendts, Sarah Manley and the team at Burberry for their sponsorship of the exhibition in London and Los Angeles. A great sponsor makes many things possible, and both the financial and creative input from Burberry are very much appreciated.

Sandy Nairne is Director of the National Portrait Gallery, London

FOREWORD
GRAYDON CARTER

In that fertile first quarter of the last century, when the new was not yet new, the incubator for what would become the Modern Age was bubbling with activity. For starters, there were those two seismic breaks with the past: the First World War and the revolution in Russia. There were the life-altering innovations of electric power, the light bulb, the household telephone, the record player, the radio, the Model T and the airplane. And smack in the middle of that quarter-century, in the more cosmopolitan drawing rooms of the globe, the talk ran to New York's 1913 Armory Show, which introduced modern art to America, and to the debut performance of Stravinsky's *The Rite of Spring*, in Paris, which introduced modern music to the world. It was also around this time that my predecessor Frank Crowninshield (not incidentally, one of the organizers of the Armory Show) was conscripted by publisher Condé Nast to edit a journal that would slip off the dusty velvet cloak of the Edwardian era and escort its readers into the fizzy, raffish affair that came to be known as the Jazz Age.

The magazine was initially called *Dress and Vanity Fair*, and in 1913 the first issue fell into the hands of New York's smart set. Within six months, Nast had wisely dropped the *Dress* from its name and brought Crowninshield aboard, and, within two years, the magazine was taking in more advertising than any other monthly in the country. By 1920 the top names on the masthead included Dorothy Parker, Robert Benchley and Robert Sherwood. By mid-decade, Edward Steichen, its principal photographer, was making $35,000 a year – this at a time when an East Side New York town house went for $40,000.

Crowninshield championed the renowned and the soon-to-be, mixing words and pictures into an intoxicating cocktail of sophistication and chic. Everybody wrote for *Vanity Fair* in those days: P.G. Wodehouse, Gertrude Stein, Aldous Huxley, D.H. Lawrence, Edmund Wilson, Noel Coward, e.e. cummings and Alexander Woollcott. But it was for its photography that *Vanity Fair* truly and indelibly made its name. Crowninshield assembled an unmatched stable of legends: Steichen certainly, but also Baron De Meyer, Nickolas Muray, Anton Bruehl, George Hoyningen-Huene, Lusha Nelson, Man Ray, Imogen Cunningham, Cecil Beaton, James Abbe, George Hurrell and Horst P. Horst. He then urged them to unclutter their images, to be bold, to be daring and to be modern.

Crowninshield's baby turns 95 this year. There was a notable 47-year period when *Vanity Fair* didn't publish, but that changed when S.I. Newhouse, Jr, relaunched the magazine, in 1983. And so Newhouse's baby also turns 25 this year. Pictures are as important a part of the mix of the current version as they were of the original. Accordingly, *Vanity Fair* has assembled a stable of photographers with Promethean talents to match Crowninshield's squad, beginning with the magazine's principal photographer, Annie Leibovitz, and including Bruce Weber, Mario Testino, Patrick Demarchelier, Mark Seliger, Mary Ellen Mark, Snowdon, Sebastião Salgado, Harry Benson, Jonathan Becker, Jonas Karlsson, James Nachtwey, Robert Mapplethorpe, Bill King, Herb Ritts, Helmut Newton and David LaChapelle.

Vanity Fair Portraits, a glorious exhibition of great work from both incarnations of the magazine – beginning with our partner, the National Portrait Gallery in London – is arguably no less than a history of portrait photography of the last century.

Graydon Carter has been the editor of Vanity Fair *since 1992*

SPONSOR'S FOREWORD
CHRISTOPHER BAILEY

It is a great privilege to be able to continue the Burberry history of supporting the arts. It is particularly exciting on this occasion to be working with the iconic magazine *Vanity Fair* and, once again, with the renowned British institution that is the National Portrait Gallery.

Vanity Fair has redefined portraiture and all that it stands for, elevating the magazine far beyond the realm of fashion. *Vanity Fair* is an institution. It has always had an extraordinary ability to offer a glimpse inside the lives of generations of talent, be they actors, musicians, politicians, artists, entrepreneurs, writers or athletes, even Her Majesty Queen Elizabeth II – a cast unrivalled by any other magazine. These images are largely the work of the acknowledged masters of photography: Helmut Newton, Cecil Beaton, Edward Steichen, Annie Leibovitz, Mario Testino and David Hockney (one of my personal idols), to name but a few. As a fashion designer, I have been inspired by many of these photographers and their creativity, and I have been fortunate enough to work closely with some of them, which has been an honour.

Great photographers are able to penetrate the outer layer of a person, to capture an unseen side and in doing so unveil a character we have never seen before. Ironically, and deservedly, photographers have now become as famous as their subjects – icons captured by icons.

There is a magic about photography. Everyone will see something different and will interpret an image in their own way. That is the beauty of it. Behind every great photo is a wonderful story: how it arose, be it by chance, fate or meticulous planning; flying from city to city to meet demanding schedules and deadlines. These tales add their own colour to the images and an extra dynamic in a seemingly static frame.

I cannot think of anywhere better than the National Portrait Gallery in London, followed by LACMA in Los Angeles, to show some of the most significant portraits ever published. This will be the third time Burberry has had the pleasure of working with the National Portrait Gallery (indeed we both celebrated our 150th anniversaries in 2006). Burberry is delighted to support *Vanity Fair Portraits* in two great cities, and to play a part in enabling these historical yet timeless images to be shared with a wider audience than ever before.

Christopher Bailey is Creative Director of Burberry

CURATORS' PREFACE
DAVID FRIEND
TERENCE PEPPER

It all began with a phone call in February 2005. And now, almost three years to the day, two key players of the photography world have collaborated to produce *Vanity Fair Portraits: Photographs 1913–2008*, an exhibition staged at the National Portrait Gallery, London, presenting 150 works in all – 95 years of portraits by more than 70 photographers as part of a three-continent tour.

The notion of an exhibition surveying a century of classic portrait photography from the pages of *Vanity Fair* had been percolating for years during discussions between the magazine's longtime editor, Graydon Carter, and its editor of creative development, David Friend. At one point, Carter said that when it came to photographic portraiture no institution in the world had the experience, knowledge and prestige of the National Portrait Gallery. At his urging, a phone call was placed to the Gallery's director, Sandy Nairne, enquiring about a possible meeting to explore a joint project: a show and a book that might be timed to coincide with the magazine's 95th anniversary in 2008 (the Jazz Age *Vanity Fair* was published from 1913 to 1936) and its 25th anniversary as a relaunched monthly.

Enthusiastically, Nairne and the National Portrait Gallery's curator of photographs, Terence Pepper, met in London with Friend, who brought along an armful of colour copies of images by an array of *Vanity Fair* photographers, from Man Ray and Edward Steichen to Helmut Newton and Annie Leibovitz. Within a few weeks, the two institutions agreed to collaborate on an exhibition that would be the first to showcase *Vanity Fair*'s rare vintage prints alongside its contemporary equivalents.

There were three principal criteria for arriving at the select 150 works presented here: photographs that are enduring or iconic (some of which have become the subjects' definitive depictions); pictures that uniquely distill the essential persona of the subject, the signature style of the photographer, or both; and outtakes, or variant poses, and lesser-known studies (some of which have not been previously displayed) that, with the passage of time, provide a fresh perspective on the sitter, the portraitist, or the period.

Pepper, who pored over back issues of the magazine and flew to New York three times to sample virtually every *Vanity Fair* photograph in the legendary Condé Nast Archive, considers the show to have fulfilled a lifetime dream. 'I had been an addict when it came to the wealth of imagery produced under the Condé Nast imprimatur,' he says. 'As far back as the mid-1970s, when I joined the National Portrait Gallery, I made my first visit to the British *Vogue* archive, where the librarian allowed me access to old bound copies of American, French and British *Vogue* and, most important, to *Vanity Fair*, for my research on a 1978 show for the 100th anniversary of the birth of photographer E.O. Hoppé. Thirty years later, viewing *Vanity Fair*'s cache of vintage pre-war prints has been a high point of my career as a photography historian.'

For Friend, the endeavour was a homecoming of sorts. During a college semester abroad, in the 1970s, he would often take the London Underground to Trafalgar Square and head to the Gallery for a visual crash course in British history. For this exhibition, Friend, the former director of photography for *Life*, reviewed every picture in all 570-plus issues of *Vanity Fair*, vintage and modern, again immersing himself in portraiture. 'It is uncanny how one publication,' he says, 'has consistently commissioned and nurtured the masters of the medium, helping to define how we view the public image of the celebrated.' Pepper concurs. '*Vanity Fair*,' he says, 'set a benchmark in portrait photography, and this exhibition attests to the significance of the magazine's visual legacy in our era.'

Taken together, these images illuminate the pivotal role of *Vanity Fair*, which, while gauging and shaping the progress and spirit of the times, has managed to promote many of the most memorable portrait photographs and photographers of the twentieth century.

THE WORLD IS A LOOKING-
GLASS, AND GIVES BACK
TO EVERY MAN THE REFLECTION
OF HIS OWN FACE.

WILLIAM MAKEPEACE THACKERAY, THE NOVEL *VANITY FAIR*, SERIALIZED IN *PUNCH*, 1847

DIVINE DECADENCE
CHRISTOPHER HITCHENS

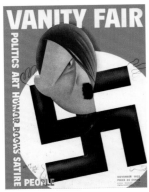

Fig.01
'The Return of the Prodigal'
Vanity Fair cover, October 1933

Fig.02
Adolf Hitler, *Vanity Fair* cover by
Paolo Garretto, November 1932

At times, *Vanity Fair* struck ominous
chords, as evidenced by these two
Depression-era covers.

'Divine decadence, darling', breathes Liza Minnelli in recommending the motto of her Berlin nightclub in Bob Fosse's *Cabaret*. The very word 'divine' seems to summon the world of Evelyn Waugh and his 'Bright Young Things', dancing until dawn and frittering their brittle lives away on the inventions of transient pleasure. 'Oh, Nina, what a lot of parties!' That's the encapsulating observation in Waugh's *Vile Bodies*, a novel where beneath the dying strains of the light music you can, as with *Cabaret*, feel the Second World War coming on. Even in *The Great Gatsby* F. Scott Fitzgerald manages a hint of the sinister undertone of the Jazz Age. 'Yellow cocktail music', he called it, in one of the most arresting images of the period. And when he referred to his protagonists as 'careless people', he didn't mean carefree. He meant that they didn't mind about anyone else.

The association between luxury and decadence, and the punishment of these by disaster, is an almost automatic one in our culture. Marie Antoinette maintains a sumptuous court while all the while the fires of resentment are being stoked to white heat. A band plays on the *Titanic* as the gowns and white ties perform their elegant combinations. The

nobles of St Petersburg look down from their brilliantly lit windows and fail to see the snarling hatred that is gathering in the darkness. The hedonism of Weimar morphs into the grin on a suppurating corpse. Or as Hilaire Belloc once put it about pre-war England: 'When they married and gave in marriage/They danced at the County Ball/And some of them kept a carriage./*And the flood destroyed them all.*'

There are certain crucial dates that encapsulate this sense of impending doom and inescapable nemesis. The year 1914 is one such: the bitter storm that put an abrupt end to what Edwardian England called 'the long garden party'. The year 1939 is yet another. In September of that year, W.H. Auden was in a gay bar in New York, brooding on the evil Europe he had left behind and saying sarcastically of those around him that for them: 'The lights must never go out, the music must always play.'

By that time, the first incarnation of *Vanity Fair* – born in 1914 (after four ill-conceived issues in 1913, under the hybrid title *Dress and Vanity Fair*), shuttered in 1936 – had already ceased to be. The temptation is to regard this, too, as some kind of verdict on frivolity.

But in fact the lights must never go out. The music must always play. Even in the darkest time, there must be beauty and style and the cultivation of taste and the individual. (The importance of the individual against the massified and the collective is, in fact, one of the most important lessons to have been imparted by the twentieth century.) And there is no time in which the celebration of irony – that cream in our coffee and gin in our Campari – is not of the first importance. It isn't as if the forces of seriousness and solemnity and ideological rectitude come very well out of Weimar, either. One of my favourite images of the midnight of the epoch is that of *Vanity Fair*'s former drama critic P.G. Wodehouse, interned by the Nazis in a disused lunatic asylum in Poland, sitting not very far from the site of Auschwitz and scribbling out *Money in the Bank*. (Appraising Upper Silesia he said to himself: 'What must Lower Silesia be like?' That's the sort of thing Oscar Wilde might have managed in the same circumstances.) The debonair, indeed, often shows itself to best advantage amid the dreariness and conformity that are the counterparts of war, dictatorship and other serious matters.

I began with Evelyn Waugh because he was one of the great

exemplars of that literary and artistic modernism (he was a deft illustrator of his own novels as well as those of other people) that provided the good fairies at the birth of the first American *Vanity Fair*. What are the signatures of this style? And why is it still called 'modern'? Well, to answer the second question first, from 1913 we start to periodize history by decades. Up until then, even for many Americans, eras were named after monarchs and reigns. In England, this practice ends with the Edwardian, which is, not coincidentally, the antechamber to the hell of the First World War and the ensuing collapse of most of the great thrones. In America, which used to periodize things like architecture with sobriquets like 'Colonial', we had already had 'the Gilded Age', followed by 'the Nineties', thus setting the scene for 'the Twenties' or 'the Jazz Age' (*Vanity Fair* was *the* Jazz Age magazine): periods that are practically co-terminous. It is, though, 'the Thirties' that confirm the idea of the decade as the modern way in which to reckon both history and culture.

To modernity, then. Without attempting an exhaustive definition, one can mention experiments with language and form, diminished respect for religion, the celebration of the fully fledged individual personality, the spread of images that are made with celluloid rather than with paint or stone, or that lend themselves to this form of reproduction, and – this perhaps above all – the loosening of sexual repression. Improvisation in music ceases to be frowned upon. Travel becomes a theme, even a need. The concept of speed is pervasive, as perhaps is the awareness of time being short. Easy money and new money are not thought of as necessarily immoral, and gambling becomes an art. (The implosion of the great casino of Wall Street in 1929 nearly replaces the *Titanic* of 1912 as the surpassing image.) Censorship, given the profusion and proliferation of means of communication, becomes almost a thing of the past. Its counterpart – Prohibition – is the occasion for something like mass civil disobedience in America, with the flaunting of the cocktail shaker and the speakeasy. Youth is to be celebrated for its own sake. An ambivalent phrase – 'the loss of innocence' – becomes familiar. People start to wise up (figs 1,2).

Frank Crowninshield's *Vanity Fair* was therefore the right magazine at the right time. And in order to have any sensitivity to timing, it is important above all to know when to stop. When to leave a party.

When to break off an affair. The effect to be achieved is this: to be asked why you are doing so rather than why you are not. Taking all things into consideration, 1936 was just the right year for *Vanity Fair* to hang up its hat. With the war in Spain beginning that summer, and the severe aesthetic of the Works Progress Administration beginning to magnetize most of the country's best photographers and writers – even the divine Miss Dorothy Parker, Wodehouse's successor as the magazine's drama critic – the best recourse for the dandy and the *flâneur* was to adopt a policy of self-effacement. It's true that the magazine was numbered among those voices that spoke of that horrible Mr Roosevelt, and that in 1933 – the year of the Reichstag fire, no less – it had spoken of Hitler as 'Handsome Adolf – A Law unto Himself'. But H.L. Mencken had given *Mein Kampf* a friendly review, and later *Time* magazine put Hitler on the cover as Man of the Year, so perhaps this offence was not especially odious. At any rate, Mr Crowninshield understood when to bow politely out: a skill never evinced by Mr Mencken or *Time* founder Mr Luce.

In its second appearance, which we may date from the editorship of first Tina Brown and then Graydon Carter, the magazine had the advantage of knowing the mistakes of the previous one. People living in Weimar didn't exactly know that it was the Weimar period they were living through, but if in the 1990s one commissioned a feature on Leni Riefenstahl, for example, one had to do so with a certain – shall we say? – irony. A moral rudder could be – not too obtrusively – felt. One of the achievements of Crowninshield had been, in the spirit of the Parisian Americans of 'the lost generation', to introduce his readers to a world beyond the shores of American isolationism. By the 1980s, the world beyond those shores had become obsessed above all by American culture. And thus the choice of two non-American editors – Brown from England, Carter from Canada – who had been drawn into the American orbit was probably not accidental. They were volunteers for what Crowninshield in his mission statement (not that he would have dreamed of calling it that) had specified as 'the progress and promise of American life'. And, even if it all seemed a touch meretricious to many of us at the time, the Reagan years did mark the beginning of a new self-reliance and the close of the epoch of quasi-statism that had begun with F.D.R.'s New Deal. To the cartoonists, Nancy Reagan

Fig.03
'9/11', photograph by
Adam Woodward
Vanity Fair, September 2002

Fig.04
President Bill Clinton and
Vice President Al Gore,
Vanity Fair cover by Annie Leibovitz,
November 1997

Fig.05
Actor and environmental activist
Leonardo DiCaprio and Knut,
a polar bear cub, *Vanity Fair* cover
by Annie Leibovitz, May 2007

The present-day magazine has
dedicated extensive coverage to the
aftermath of the 2001 terror attacks
and produced special issues devoted
to subjects as varied as the world's
power elite and the environment.

might sometimes have resembled Marie Antoinette, but there were a lot of blue-collar Reaganites about, and it certainly showed.

I shall not easily forget the time, in 1994, when those voters showed their power again and gave Congressman Newt Gingrich control of the US House of Representatives. It fell to me to ask his press secretary, Tony Blankley, if the new Speaker and his closest cohort would agree to a group photograph for *Vanity Fair*. No thanks, was roughly the response. I pressed him. Perhaps he did not appreciate, I said, that the magazine was read not just by moguls, socialites and Hollywood types. It had millions of readers in the middle of the nation as well. 'Oh, yes, we do know that,' replied Blankley (himself a former Hollywood child actor). 'And it's those very people we don't want to see us in your glossy pages.' I thought that this postmodern rebuff contained a distinct if oblique compliment. Anyway, it wasn't long before all Republicans were more than willing to be found posing in our pages once more. And it's been some time now since I have seen the magazine dismissed, in lofty tones, as being 'glitzy' or a 'glossy'.

'If I say someone has no sense of humour,' my friend Martin Amis once remarked, 'I mean above all to impugn his seriousness.' Grasp this, and you have the root of the matter. I spent half my life working for grimly 'serious' weeklies like *The Nation*, and I sometimes turn straight to Edwin Coaster when I get my new copy of *Vanity Fair*, but it is on the magazine's behalf that I have found myself standing on mass graves in Eritrea, watching the ebb and flow of combat in Iraq and Afghanistan, talking to persecuted dissenters in Cuba and chronicling the effects of chemical warfare in Vietnam. To have once or twice worked with photographers like James Nachtwey is to have appreciated the way in which – contrary to a once cherished belief of mine – the photographic image can possess a moral weight greater than words. But there is no shame in returning from such an assignment and reporting to an office where fashion and comedy are also given a lot of loving attention. If I were to feel particularly sententious, I might even say that these are among the things in our culture that make it worth defending, against a stone-faced monotheistic and monochrome barbarism. Irony is another of these virtues – precisely because it is the polar opposite of the literal and humourless mind-set – and I

think that Carter was fairly quick to see that he had been flirting with a false antithesis when he made his famous remark that 11 September 2001 marked the end of the age of irony.

Vanity Fair had never shirked the serious before September 2001, devoting huge space to Africa, for example, in 1994, the year that saw both the genocide in Rwanda and the election of Nelson Mandela to the presidency of South Africa. It devoted impressive attention, too, to the AIDS crisis, beginning with a feature in 1988 that curtain-raised the now regular idea of the 'special issue'. But it's probably not wrong to say that after 2001 the magazine became more self-conscious in emphasizing investigations, warnings, and the grainy and gritty aspects of modern life (figs 3,4,5), while never ceasing to 'own' the coverage of entertainment, media and ephemeral quirkiness. Two very salient matters are set to dominate discussion for the next decade at the very least: the climatic crisis and the war on, or with, another, and theocratic, worldview. Not only can the magazine be counted upon to bring news from both fronts in every issue, but it has also become highly identified with a critique of each phenomenon. (I can say this as one who largely

VANITY FAIR

THE
LEADERS
WHO SHAPE AND RULE
THE WORLD TODAY

SPECIAL
REPORT

A PORTRAIT OF
WORLD
POWER

INCLUDING: BILL CLINTON,
AL GORE, TONY BLAIR,
BILL GATES, GIANNI AGNELLI,
POPE JOHN PAUL II,
MADELEINE ALBRIGHT
AND MORE...

PLUS: AMERICA,
THE LAST EMPIRE
BY GORE VIDAL

ALSO:
LESLIE BENNETTS on ELTON JOHN,
ROBERT SAM ANSON on SEYMOUR HERSH
AND EDWARD KLEIN on ATHINA ONASSIS ROUSSEL

concurs with his colleagues about the planetary warming emergency, and who sharply disagrees with most of them – and in the pages of *Vanity Fair*, at that – about the conflict in Iraq.)

These considerations even influence the relationship of the magazine to the all-important word 'party'. Frank Crowninshield conceived of *Vanity Fair* as a gathering of all that was witty and sophisticated, sure to 'ignite a dinner party at fifty yards'. Tina Brown – who had published a collection of essays called *Life as a Party* before becoming editor – dreamed of getting all the most amusing people into one room and then plying them with drinks to see what would happen. She also ran a memoir of depression, *Darkness Visible*, by William Styron, who once told me that it was parties, above all parties in his own honour, which drove him to turn his thoughts to suicide. Evelyn Waugh would have known what he meant. 'Oh, Nina, what a lot of parties!'

Vanity Fair has now quite transcended the café society of its earlier incarnation. On one night of the year, it dominates Hollywood with an enviable reception. On another, it has the whole attention of the Cannes Film Festival with what it would be otiose to call a hot ticket. On still

another, it is, again, the cream in the coffee and the gin in the Campari on what would otherwise be the rather flat evening of the White House Correspondents' Association Dinner, in Washington. But on any other given night, at a party for the Natural Resources Defense Council, for example, or for Darfur and Not On Our Watch, the best table at the fund-raising event is likely to feature not just the magazine's business side, but also the presence of writers and photographers who actually know about these matters at first hand. Mr Crowninshield's best-known descendant is his great-nephew, Benjamin Crowninshield Bradlee, the legendary editor of the *Washington Post* at the time of Watergate, and the man who can fairly be credited with ending the tenure of a sick and venal president. Graydon Carter's raging thirst to emulate him in this respect may never quite be slaked, but all hard-news journalists in my hometown of Washington now read *Vanity Fair* as a matter of course, and more of them would like to write for it than can easily be accommodated. I don't think Mr Crowninshield ever quite contrived to be able to say that.

Looking back over the elegant and polished issues that he published in the inter-war decades,

I was struck more than anything by the way that the advertisements consisted largely of words. A lot of quite pretty and persuasive writing was done, in those days, by agency copywriters. (Even in our own time, both Salman Rushdie and Martin Amis got a start in the language game by producing material like this for Madison Avenue.)

Now, though, it is the work of photography upon which almost all advertising relies, and it used to be fashionable to complain that with *Vanity Fair* it had become hard to tell where the ads ended and the articles began. That this was unjust can easily be demonstrated, as Terence Pepper and David Friend show in their expert essays (pp.18–37; pp.120–135) on the immense care that true non-commercial photography requires, and the startling frames and framings that are the result. There's no doubt as to which archive of the lens a future social historian will have to consult.

The word 'magazine', as I never tire of saying, has three other distinct but related meanings. It connotes, first, the French word *magasin*, or store, or shop. It implies, second, a chamber of cartridges that feed automatically into the breech of a gun. And, third, it is the 'magazine' in which powder and ammunition are kept. In one instance, it's a distinction rather

than a disclaimer to be able to boast that one contains or carries something to suit almost every customer; in the others, it's good to be able to claim that one will not run out of shot, or shots. This is not the same as being all things to all people. I tend to skip, for example, the numerous articles about real or pretended monarchs, an aspect of celebrity journalism that links the Crowninshield, Brown and Carter editions. But I don't say that the subject isn't of intrinsic interest. In return, I hope that those who like to read about royal families will stay to learn about the elemental struggle in the Niger Delta, say, to name only one essay from 2007 – by Sebastian Junger – that I enviously wish I had written myself.

Globalization requires that one be simultaneously omnivorous and discriminating. There has to be something between the instant coffee of television, the 'first draft' of the daily press, the uncheckable plethora of the blogs and the longer file of the book. Monthly magazine journalism, allowing one to register the shock of the new while daring to give space to historians, is arguably the golden mean for those who want to keep up and also to take a step back. They had it easy in those 'Roaring Twenties'.

VANITY FAIR PORTRAITS 1913-36

VANITY FAIR WAS ...
AS ACCURATE A SOCIAL
BAROMETER OF ITS TIME
AS EXISTS.

CLEVELAND AMORY, SOCIAL CRITIC, 1960

THE PORTRAIT PHOTOGRAPH IN THE MODERN AGE
TERENCE PEPPER

06

07

Fig.06
Mme Pavlova in *Le Cygne*,
Dress and Vanity Fair cover by
Schneider of Berlin, December 1913

Fig.07
Broadway actor Clifton Webb,
comedian Jimmy Savo as *sommelier*
and film star Irene Dunne, *Vanity Fair*
cover by Anton Bruehl, July 1934

The launch of *Vanity Fair* by the visionary publisher Condé Nast coincided with the birth of modernism, the dawning of the Jazz Age and the mould-breaking 1913 Armory Show that introduced avant-garde art to the American public. Nast, together with editor Frank Crowninshield, wanted to create a magazine that would engage with this vibrant modern culture, that would not only comment upon but also champion all that was at the forefront of change and innovation in the arts.

It was to be a magazine in tune with its time. *Vanity Fair* became a cultural catalyst, promoting the work of contemporary artists and illustrators (such as Pablo Picasso and Constantin Brancusi in the 1910s, and Miguel Covarrubias and Paolo Garretto in the 1920s and 1930s), publishing essays by new literary talents (from Dorothy Parker and Gertrude Stein to D.H. Lawrence and Aldous Huxley), and upholding the genre of celebrity portraiture through the progressive work of photographers such as Baron De Meyer, Edward Steichen, Man Ray and Cecil Beaton. It was this world that *Vanity Fair* defined for its cosmopolitan, glittering audience, and which was both reflected and celebrated in its informative, sophisticated and sometimes irreverent pages.

If the magazine was the messenger, then photography was its dominant medium. In its golden early years *Vanity Fair* was the showcase for what was to become the most accessible art form in twentieth-century America, commissioning the work of the greatest photographers of the era. From the very first issues photographers were profiled alongside artists and writers, and the fees paid to secure the top talents of the time were impressively fulsome.

There are two principal star photographers in the early history of *Vanity Fair*: Baron De Meyer and Edward Steichen. But their work was significantly boosted by a large roster of other master photographers – including names such as Charles Sheeler, Nickolas Muray, Anton Bruehl, George Hoyningen-Huene, Lusha Nelson, Imogen Cunningham and Baroness Tony Von Horn – whose commissioned photography helped visually to set the tone for the magazine as a whole.

Nast and Crowninshield: A Meeting of Minds

Vanity Fair was the creation of two exceptional men: Condé Montrose Nast (1873–1942) and Frank Crowninshield (1872–1947).[1] Condé Nast had established his publishing credentials at *Collier's Weekly*. The son of a broker and one-time American attaché in Stuttgart and a banker's daughter, Nast graduated from Georgetown University in 1894 and went on to attend law school at Washington University in St Louis in 1897. While at Georgetown, he met fellow college pupil Robert Collier, who was heir to the title's ownership. As advertising and business manager for the magazine between 1898 and 1907 Nast increased its circulation from just under 20,000 in 1897 to over half a million ten years later. From this powerful position Nast purchased his first magazine in 1909, *Vogue*. The title had been founded in 1892 as a small-scale New York high-society social gazette. Nast remodelled it and found ways to attract a higher level of quality advertising so that, under the editorship of Edna Woolman Chase, it became a highly sophisticated and profitable brand-leading fashion magazine. *Vogue*'s profits mushroomed: $5,000 in 1909, $400,000 in 1915, $650,000 in 1929, the year of the stock market crash; over the same period circulation boomed, growing from 30,000 to over 140,000 copies a month.

Four years after his purchase of *Vogue*, Nast bought *Dress*, which he saw as a potential *Vogue* rival, and paid $3,000 for the rights to a slightly lowbrow gossip and theatre-oriented magazine with a famous title, *Vanity Fair*.[2] Combining the two, he launched his first issue of *Dress and Vanity Fair* in September 1913 with the strapline 'Fashions – the Stage, Society, Sports, The Fine Arts'. The editorial in the first issue stated that the goal of the magazine was to 'touch on all that is of interest in the Drama, the Opera, and Music, both at home and in Europe. We shall discuss all that is new and worthy in the Fine Arts and in Books … We shall not lack authority in those things which go to make the smart world smart.'

This was indeed the era of the 'smart magazine' and Nast wanted to follow in the wake of the already established literary title edited by H.L. Mencken, *The Smart Set* (1900–1929). Nast had evolved a theory that the formula for a successful magazine was less about attracting the largest number of readers and more to do with addressing the interests of a particular group, which advertisers would pay money to reach. His intention was to produce a 'class publication' that would appeal not only to the moneyed, established and intelligent American upper class but also to those who aspired to be part of it.

His newly fashioned hybrid, however, was not the vehicle with which to achieve his ambitions. Unhappy with the first few issues of *Dress and Vanity Fair* Nast looked for advice to Frank Crowninshield, then working as art editor for *Century Magazine*, who replied that the magazine was too similar to the fashion-led *Vogue*: 'There is no magazine that is read by the people you meet at lunches and dinners. Your magazine should cover the things people talk about … parties, the arts, sports, theatre, humor, and so forth.' With this Nast recognized a meeting of minds and Crowninshield's potential to create a magazine that would promote avant-garde ideas within the context of an aspirational and multi-arts agenda, whilst retaining a foundation of establishment values.

Nast at once appointed Crowninshield as editor and agreed to drop the first half of the original title. Issue five appeared renamed as *Vanity Fair* in January 1914.[3] Throughout its 22-year incarnation, the magazine's circulation hovered between 85,000 and 95,000 and although in 1915 it earned more from advertising than any other American monthly, very few issues reportedly made a profit. Nast's attachment to the title placed editorial excellence above all else and he was able to subsidize its high production values due to the financial success of his other periodicals.

Like Nast, Crowninshield was a man about town with a keen interest in the arts. His cultural tastes had been shaped by his father Frederic, a Boston-born watercolourist and mural painter who had taught art in Paris and Rome.

Born in Paris and educated in Europe, Crowninshield travelled to New York to begin a literary career that started as a clerk at Putnam's. In 1895 he became publisher of the New York literary review the *Bookman*, followed by an assistant editorship at *Metropolitan Magazine* until 1902. Other literary work took him to London in 1908 and 1909, where he negotiated rights to buy magazine stories for the huge readership (in excess of 500,000) of *Munsey's Magazine*.

In 1913 Frank Crowninshield acted as an unpaid and unofficial publicity agent for the International Exhibition of Modern Art, held at the 69th Regiment Armory in New York, of which Alfred Stieglitz, father of art photography in America, was Honorary Vice-President. The Armory Show was later seen as a watershed event in awakening America to Europe's modernist ideas and Marcel Duchamp's *Nude Descending a Staircase* became a much-reviled *cause célèbre*. The show attracted over 300,000 visitors and helped define the start of a new 'modernist' period in the arts. (An art connoisseur, Crowninshield would go on to become one of the seven co-founders of the Museum of Modern Art, established in 1929.)

Not only would Crowninshield help Nast to achieve his vision for *Vanity Fair*. He would also help him to nurture Manhattan's 'café society'. Nast would throw parties that brought together the talented, the rich and the beautiful from the spheres of literature, the arts, sports, politics, cinema and high society. Throughout the 1920s and into the 1930s, *Vanity Fair* set the standard for the 'smart' magazines of the era.

New York – London

In his first issue as editor Crowninshield had stated a wish 'to pattern *Vanity Fair* in a general way, after the great English pictorial weeklies, [which] has been our aim from the start. We feel

08

Fig.08
'Dolores – Personifying the Spirit
of Vanity' by Baron De Meyer
Vanity Fair, December 1919

Born Kathleen Rose, the six-foot-tall,
British-born fashion model Dolores
is shown in her second career as
a spectacularly dressed Ziegfeld
Follies dancer in this signed and
elaborately presented composition.
De Meyer had previously taken
fashion photographs of Dolores, who
had worked with the House of Lucile,
founded by Lady Duff Gordon.

we have gained an excellent idea of the kind of English magazines Americans want.' It was the English weekly founded by Thomas Gibson Bowles in 1868 that provided some of the inspiration for the new American creation. The London-based magazine, which finally closed in February 1914, had considerable literary content but more memorably ran a series of collectable lithographic caricatures produced by a diverse collection of artists.[4] Its first subjects were the politicians Gladstone and Disraeli.[5] A plethora of categories followed including Actors and Theatrical Managers, Americans, Cricketers, Indian Princes, Jockeys and Judges through to Yachtsmen.[6] The ethos of the American magazine that followed in its footsteps, that of mixing and matching personalities from different classes and creeds, took its lead from its British predecessor. And this was nowhere better expressed than in the work of the Mexican-born illustrator and caricaturist Miguel Covarrubias, who joined the magazine in 1923, aged only 19. He produced many memorable cover portraits and a long series of 'Impossible Interviews'. These comprised imaginary pairings of such unlikely contenders as Greta Garbo and Calvin Coolidge, Sigmund Freud and Jean Harlow, and Clark

Gable and the Prince of Wales.

The editor was not only taking his cues from the United Kingdom. He was borrowing from France as well, where modernism was flourishing. In the magazine's 1914 mission statement, Crowninshield insisted that his journal would 'wean [American photographers, authors and illustrators] from their stiff, unyielding ways and make them, as the French periodicals have succeeded in making theirs, a little more free in their technique … even absurd.' As Paris was one of the main cultural draws of the Jazz Age, a finger on the pulse of all things French was essential.

A New Hall of Fame

The content of the magazine was key and the most significant new feature to be introduced, in December 1913, was 'Snap Shots for the Hall of Fame', a page of written profiles accompanied by well-chosen photographs. This was to become a central part of the magazine, providing a vehicle for talent spotting and the introduction of new names. Among the first subjects were Anna Pavlova, 'the greatest dancer of the age', Arnold Henry Savage Landor, 'the first European traveler to enter the forbidden city of Tibet [*sic*]',

and Auguste Rodin, 'at work in his atelier'. Subsequent 'snap shots' in 1914 included a specially commissioned photograph of Irving Berlin from Brown Brothers (p.43) and the Russian ballet designer Leon Bakst. Later, the series was renamed 'We Nominate for the Hall of Fame' and helped introduce cutting-edge or emerging artists, designers, authors and film directors to a wider audience. In the modern incarnation of *Vanity Fair*, the Hall of Fame feature would be continued, adopted sometimes as a single page, often as an annual pictorial portfolio, surveying the outstanding personalities, visionaries and newsmakers of the year.

Creating the Look

What gave *Vanity Fair* its particular identity as it developed, however, was not only its literary voice, lively attitude and sharp wit, but also its design. Crowninshield, largely responsible for overseeing the stylish and elegant layout, sought to replicate the high standards found in the pages of the *Tatler* and the *Sketch*, where photographs by leading British photographers such as E.O. Hoppé and Malcolm

Arbuthnot often appeared in tinted photogravure reproduction. What was exceptional from the very beginning in *Vanity Fair* was the reverential way in which portraits were published on the page, with wide white margins to signify their importance as photographic art. Photographers were clearly credited.

The accomplished illustrator Heyworth Campbell was created art director of *Vogue* in 1909 and thereafter became the main designer for all Nast's magazines until his resignation in 1927. At *Vogue* he established an editorial-advertising-design mix that was calculated to attract a highly specialized audience, appealing to their particular interests with a unique combination of ingredients. This ethos he brought to *Vanity Fair*. Apart from two photographic covers in 1913 (fig.6) and a further three (in colour) in the 1930s (fig.7), a tradition of graphic covers was established, using coloured illustrations by artists such as Helen Dryden, 'Fish' (Anne Harriet Fish), Georges Lepape and A.E. Marty. But even though Campbell appeared to be in charge overall, Crowninshield wielded considerable control over the look of each page, drawing diagrams to show how large a picture should be reproduced, or

how many columns of type should be used.

Once modernism was in full swing in the 1920s, the magazine underwent further graphic adjustments. *Vanity Fair* illustrator Eduardo Benito, based in Paris, fully embraced the new styles of 'moderne' design and typography presented at the 1925 Paris Exposition that launched Art Deco. His recommendations on clarity, legibility and modernity were applied to Nast's magazines but Benito turned down the chance to become Campbell's successor. Instead this mantle was taken on by a Turkish-born designer, Mehemed Fehmy Agha (1896–1978), who was working in Berlin on German *Vogue* and was able to implement, and extend, Benito's modernist ideas.

In 1929 Dr Agha, as he was known, was recruited to New York as the new art director of Nast's stable of magazines, with the particular brief to redesign *Vanity Fair*. Agha, like Campbell before him, had first proved himself with *Vogue*, by showing that the art director was an integral part of the editorial process. A pioneer of the use of sans serif typefaces, the duotone, full-colour photographs and bled images, with *Vanity Fair* he made bold use of white space, banished

italics, placed photographs asymmetrically on the page and even designed an entire issue with no capital letters. It was under his direction that the first double-page spread was introduced in 1930.

Art and Photography

In the 1920s, modernism, which had been a minority taste before the First World War, came to define the age. It was seen in Europe in such major art movements as Dada, Constructivism and Surrealism, as well as in smaller developments such as that of the Bloomsbury Group. Breaking with the concept of national schools, artists and writers adopted the ideas of these international movements, which rapidly found supporters far beyond their original geographic base. Artists and writers, musicians and dancers were now emanating from Paris, Berlin and London as well as the East and West Coasts of the United States. When Nast set up foreign editions of *Vogue* (British *Vogue* in 1916, then French *Vogue* in 1920 and briefly German *Vogue*, which closed after an inauspicious launch and only a few issues in April 1928), this gave the American edition and *Vanity Fair*

access to the best artists and photographers in each country.

A passion for the modern art movement was evident in the pages of *Vanity Fair* from the outset. It promoted the often controversial work of contemporary artists before any other magazine did so, frequently to loud cries of outrage. 'We were ten years too early [in 1915] in talking to people about Van Gogh, Gauguin, Matisse, Picasso etc,' Nast later commented, admitting that this enthusiasm may not always have been helpful to the advertisers being sought for the magazine. Aristide Maillol, Marie Laurencin, Kees van Dongen and Jacob Epstein also found their way into the pages of the publication.

This influence manifested itself in other ways. Many of *Vanity Fair*'s early photographers had trained as painters. Man Ray, a pioneer of Dadaism and the magazine's Paris photographer, had a foot in both worlds – art and photography. Cecil Beaton's first work for *Vogue* was as an illustrator, writer and caricaturist; later, in addition to photography, he designed costumes and stage and film sets. Edward Steichen was an established curator and artist and, along with Baron De Meyer, George Hoyningen-Huene

09

Fig.09
Lillian Gish, 'Like Pensive Beauty
Smiling in Her Tears', in her role
as Lucy Burrows in *Broken Blossoms*,
by Baron De Meyer
Vanity Fair, August 1919

Fig.10
Frank Danby by E.O. Hoppé,
Vanity Fair, November 1915

Hoppé's Secessionist-styled portrait
of the cigarette-smoking novelist
Julia Frankau, who wrote under
the pseudonym Frank Danby, was
one of six subjects nominated for
the November 1915 Hall of Fame.
The dry wit of the caption perfectly
illustrates why this feature was so
successful. Danby was nominated
'Because she is one of the most
entertaining of modern English
novelists. Because she is a great
authority on mezzotints. Because her
brother wrote Floradora.
Because she once managed the
Uppman Cigar Company. Because
her weekly dinners are the most
amusing in London. Because she
wrote "The Heart of a Child", and
finally because she always prided
herself (wrongly) on being a top
hole poker player.'

and others, took fashion and
advertising photographs.

The Baron De Meyer Years

Baron De Meyer (1868–1949)
had first exhibited his photographic
portraits internationally whilst still
living in Germany. By 1895 he was
established in London, a member
of the fashionable Jewish set that
formed part of the social circle of
the Prince and Princess of Wales
(the future King Edward VII and
Queen Alexandra), of whom he
made elegant and striking
portraits. Then in 1913, having
become one of the most significant
masters of the camera, De Meyer
was hired by Nast as his leading
photographer. He signed a
contract for $100 a week to work
exclusively for Nast's magazines:
for *Vogue* he would produce
fashion, still lifes and society
portraits; for *Vanity Fair* he would
photograph luminaries of the
theatre, dance and opera.
    De Meyer, the magazine's
first star photographer, was given
generous space to reproduce his
elaborate upper-case signature in
the style of the Vienna Secessionists
(figs 8, 9). Early full-page
studies for *Vanity Fair* appeared
from March 1914 and his first three
subjects were actress Ethel Levey,

opera singer Lina Cavalieri
and society figure Mrs Benjamin
Guinness. His study of Nijinsky as
the Golden Slave in *Schéhérazade*
(p.40), published in May 1916 to
coincide with the Russian dancer's
appearance in New York but
taken earlier in London, is one of
the acknowledged masterworks
amongst his many ballet studies.
    De Meyer's legacy was to
enhance the dramatic possibilities
of portraiture, especially through
his use of lighting. The backlighting
in his study for *Vanity Fair* of
George Arliss (p.48), the British-
born but American-based
actor, draws attention to the
sitter's signature monocle, whilst
the highlighting behind Charlie
Chaplin's head lends the actor
a sense of gravitas (p.49).
Chaplin was known worldwide
through his screen and print
representations, but De Meyer's
skill raises the subject's status in this
carefully constructed portrait.

The Photo-Secessionists:
Hutchinson and Genthe

In the early 1900s a group of
photographers led by Alfred
Stieglitz (1864–1946) had
formed the Photo-Secession
Group with the aim of raising
photography, initially in the

soft-focused pictorialist style, to
the same level of appreciation in
America as painting and sculpture.
They published their pictures in
Camera Work, Stieglitz's exquisitely
produced photographic journal,
and held exhibitions in the Little
Galleries of the Photo-Secession
at 291 Fifth Avenue, New York
(later known simply as 291),
created and run by Stieglitz and
Edward Steichen from 1905 to
1917. Stieglitz later used this space
to introduce to the United States
the early modernist works of
European artists such as Henri
Matisse, Auguste Rodin, Henri
Rousseau, Paul Cezanne and
Pablo Picasso.
    Perhaps one of the most
significant masters of photography
to emerge from the group had
been De Meyer, whose work
had been championed through
291. Another photographer
who contributed to the magazine
and was inspired by the Photo-
Secession Group was the
Chicago-based photographer
Eugene Hutchinson (1880–1957).
    In 1915 *Vanity Fair* profiled
Pavlova using a photograph by
Hutchinson, which he made when
her ballet company performed
in Chicago during an American
tour. He also made memorable
portraits of her while she was in
Chicago for the making of the film

The Dumb Girl of Portici (1916), including an image that shows the dancer in costume for the Danse Espagnol – her name appears in the plate at the top of the composition, written in Secessionist style. This photograph and his May 1914 portrait of war poet Rupert Brooke, subsequently published in *Vanity Fair*, have since become two of Hutchinson's most famous sittings. He later moved to New York and became an industrial photographer in the style of Charles Sheeler and Margaret Bourke-White, but while Hutchinson was still in Chicago in the 1920s, George Hurrell, one of the last contributors to the early *Vanity Fair*, became his pupil.

Arnold Genthe (1869–1942), another photographer in the Photo-Secession Group, was among the most consistent contributors to the early *Vanity Fair*. This German-born philologist-turned-photographer came to America in 1895 and made his name first through his photographs of San Francisco, in particular those of the devastation caused by the 1906 earthquake. In 1911, on moving to New York, he became better known for his portraits of dancers and theatre stars, taken in a pictorialist style, such as that of the gossamer-wrapped American dancer Margaret Severn, whom

he photographed on the beach (p.59).

By contrast his most notable image is the strictly formal group portrait of the 'Russian Masters' (p.52), which features five illustrious Russians – two actors, a director, a painter and an opera star – all eminent in their chosen fields. All visited New York at the same time to coincide with the opening of the Russian exhibition at the Brooklyn Museum and the unveiling of a Pavlova portrait by Sorine. This celebrated painting, and another he made of Queen Elizabeth, wife of King George VI, later appeared as full-colour reproductions in the magazine as part of the long-running series of 'Masterworks'. Genthe was also known for his numerous studies of members of Isadora Duncan's dance company and for some of the earliest published photographs of Greta Garbo, which appeared in *Vanity Fair* at the beginning of her meteoric and mysterious career.

Anglophile Tastes: Hoppé and Arbuthnot

Crowninshield's anglophile tastes are reflected in the British bias in *Vanity Fair*'s coverage of the arts. Two of the most prominent photographers in London covering

the arts in the 1910s were E.O. Hoppé and Malcolm Arbuthnot. Hoppé (1878–1972) was born in Munich but arrived in London in 1900. Whilst working at the Deutsche Bank he pursued his amateur interest in photography and after winning a number of prizes took up photography professionally in 1907, opening his first studio near Barons Court. His rapid success saw him chosen to represent Great Britain with Benjamin Stone at the 1909 International Exhibition of Photography in Dresden, and in the following year he held his first critically acclaimed one-man show at the Royal Photographic Society, the same year in which he co-founded the London Salon of Photography.

By 1913 his commercial and artistic success as a portraitist enabled him to occupy a large house and studio at 7 Cromwell Place, which was once the home of the successful Pre-Raphaelite artist Sir John Everett Millais.

Hoppé's iconic studies of Thomas Hardy (p.47) and Henry James, taken for the British edition of the *Bookman*, were published in early issues of *Vanity Fair*, together with his portraits of Arthur Conan Doyle and George Bernard Shaw, and his 'New Woman' study of Julia Frankau, the female author

who used the pen-name Frank Danby (fig.10), whom he shows smoking and looking confident in a manly bookish pose. Hoppé made short visits to New York between 1919 and 1921, during which he made a study of Willa Cather (p.46), which was published in the October 1921 issue and was one of several taken in a studio he used on 57th Street. (With studios in both London and New York, Hoppé prefigured the careers of later continent-swapping photographers such as Harry Benson, Helmut Newton and Annie Leibovitz.)

Hoppé was later to turn to cityscape and landscape photography, touring the United States from coast to coast; one of his seascapes was reproduced in *Vanity Fair* in 1935.[7]

Just as the young Hoppé had art lessons in the Munich studio of painter Hans von Bartels, a student of Franz von Lenbach, so his fellow Briton Malcolm Arbuthnot (1874–1968) began his training in the art world before turning to photography. Arbuthnot was elected in 1907 to the Linked Ring, the British arm of the Photo-Secession Group, and through this group he became acquainted with fellow members such as Alvin Langdon Coburn, F.H. Evans and George Bernard Shaw, who

The Best Known Actress in the World

Fig.11
Mary Pickford, 'The Best Known
Actress in the World', by Ira L. Hill
Vanity Fair, October 1915

Fig.12
Douglas Fairbanks, Sr and
Mary Pickford by Nickolas Muray
Vanity Fair, December 1922

Fig.13
'Mary Pickford Grown Up'
by Edward Steichen
Vanity Fair, September 1928

Vanity Fair charted the success
of actress Mary Pickford throughout
her career, in 1928 announcing
her return to Broadway after twenty
years in Hollywood.

was an amateur photographer as well as playwright. In 1914, showing both his avant-garde and more conventional outlook, Arbuthnot had signed the Vorticist manifesto 'Blast' and established a Bond Street portrait studio, which continued until 1926. Here he specialized in portraying figures from the arts – painters, writers, actresses and dancers – including Frank Brangwyn (published in July 1915), William Orpen (1916) and Irene Castle (1919), followed by Joseph Conrad, fellow 'Blast' signatory Ezra Pound, Henri Matisse, George Bernard Shaw (p.55) and Augustus John (p.45), all published in 1920.

Orpen, the Anglo-Irish Edwardian portraitist whom *Vanity Fair* captioned 'the most popular portrait painter of Great Britain', is shown intimately captured at home in his slippers, set off by the black-and-white-squared linoleum floor, with a glimpse of the convex mirror that he used as a prop in several celebrated self-portraits (p.44). Arbuthnot lectured on Post-Impressionism with the critic and writer Roger Fry, who later wrote art reviews for *Vanity Fair*; and through his friendship with William Nicholson his interest in painting increased, taking precedence over his photographic career, which then came to a dramatic end

when his studio and negatives were consumed in a fire. His principal artistic legacy survives only in his paintings, held in public collections including the Tate, London.

The Celebrity Portrait and the Rise of Hollywood

While *Vanity Fair* from the outset established an international perspective, it did not do so to the detriment of home-grown artistic developments. Hollywood and its social scene were to be key components of the magazine.

One of the photographs published in the first issue of the magazine was of Johnston Forbes Robertson – the revered Shakespearean actor-manager – in an early film production of *Hamlet*. This portrait by Lizzie Caswall Smith anticipated the gradual cultural shift from theatre to film that was to occur in the early twentieth century. The magazine was perfectly placed to chronicle the evolving iconography of the cinema within the context of the arts as a whole. The first film magazines had started to appear in 1911, with *Motion Picture Story* and *Photoplay*, followed by the publicity still in 1913. By assigning the more significant photographers of the day to portray the early

stars of the medium, and by placing their portraits in proximity to those of eminent writers, artists and sportsmen, *Vanity Fair* aggrandized its leading players and subsequently its auteurs and instigators – the film directors and producers.

Mary Pickford, star of the silent screen, film-maker and producer, was the first female actress to earn a million dollars and is a key figure in the history of modern celebrity. Discovered by the director D.W. Griffith, she had appeared in early films from 1909 but it was only during an appearance in a Broadway play in 1913[8] that she finally decided to commit herself to the motion picture. Subsequent successes, such as *Tess of the Storm Country* (1914) and *Rags* (1915), pushed her fame to stratospheric heights. The photographic portraits of Pickford that appeared in *Vanity Fair* encapsulate the work of some of the best photographers of the era. They ranged from her first full-page portrait by Ira L. Hill, specially commissioned for the October 1915 issue (fig.11), when she was declared 'Best Known Actress in the World', through to the 1920 official study by De Meyer of Pickford in her wedding gown prior to her marriage to Douglas Fairbanks, Sr, which she distributed widely to her

SEPTEMBER, 1925

Mary Pickford Grown Up
The Film Favourite Has Finally Staged a Successful Rebellion Against Little Girl Rôles

friends. This was followed by a joint study of the couple by Nickolas Muray, Fairbanks's occasional fencing partner and fellow bon vivant, of 1922 (fig.12), in which they are depicted in profile as the reigning King and Queen of Hollywood. In 1927 Pickford posed for Steichen under a sunshade in California (fig.13), and once again in 1934 for one final photograph.

Nickolas Muray (1892–1965) had emigrated from Hungary to the United States on the eve of the First World War and he found work in the photo-engraving department at Condé Nast. After a few years there he left to forge a photography career, opening his first New York studio in Greenwich Village in 1920 and making over 10,000 portraits over the next twenty years for a variety of magazines. It was to Muray's New York studio that the British-born novelist and *Vanity Fair* contributor D.H. Lawrence was sent for an early sitting (p.57). Muray was then despatched to London by *Vanity Fair* to photograph H.G. Wells, George Bernard Shaw and John Galsworthy, and then to Giverny in June 1926 to make a study of Claude Monet (p.94). The magazine paid tribute to the founder of French Impressionism six months before he died. Eight years after Muray's 1921 study

of the newly married Pickford and Fairbanks on a beach in Santa Monica, he captured in profile Fairbanks's son with his new wife, Joan Crawford, resting her head on his back, which became one of Muray's most seductive images (p.76).

In contrast, the career of the American-born James Abbe (1883–1973) followed a different trajectory. With the encouragement of Frank Crowninshield, who had viewed his early portfolio, Abbe moved to New York in 1917 and opened a fifth-floor studio in New York at 15 West 67th Street. Here he began photographing the stars of the New York stage. His portrait of the opera diva Amelita Galli-Curci was the first to appear full page in the October 1918 issue while other portraits of stars from the Ziegfeld Follies, such as Dolores and Kyra, made Abbe a regular contributor – by 1923 he was included in *Vanity Fair*'s list of the top ten 'Master American Portrait Photographers' and profiled in the magazine.

By then, however, Abbe had moved with the prevailing trend from theatre to film, and was taking pictures at D.W. Griffith's East Coast studios at Mamaroneck, outside New York. His most memorable studies are of the

Gish sisters on the set of *Orphans of the Storm* (p.50) and prior to that of Lillian Gish in Griffith's seminal films *Broken Blossoms* (1919) and *Way Down East* (1920). When she set off for Italy to film *The White Sister* (1923), Abbe was invited to accompany the production team as official photographer. Previously in 1920 he had travelled to Hollywood to capture first Mary Pickford and then Charlie Chaplin. After the completion of *The White Sister* Abbe made his base in Paris, where he photographed European-based stars such as the Dolly Sisters and Ida Rubinstein for *Vanity Fair* and other magazines, travelling in 1926 to London to capture fellow American expatriates Fred and Adele Astaire, who were appearing in the show *Lady Be Good* (p.51).

'Bigoted Feminists'

Amongst a multitude of directives aimed at its potential readership, the magazine's March 1914 editorial stated: 'We hereby announce ourselves as determined and bigoted feminists'. It committed itself to including intellectually appealing ideas aimed at women, which few other magazines then provided.

The publication reflected the rise of new female role models. Writers and singers as well as stars of the opera, theatre and dance worlds proliferated in the early days. *Vanity Fair* also celebrated women scientists, such as Marie Curie, and sportswomen including athletes, tennis players, swimmers and high-board divers, as well as adventurers like Amelia Earhart (p.80). Film-making created new possibilities. Mary Pickford embodied the 'new woman', healthy, robust and self-reliant. She combined sexual allure with chastity as America's sweetheart. The first star to produce her own film, Pickford was emancipated and even suffragist, sometimes using her characters to question the female position in both the family and the workplace.

Another role model of the 1920s was Gloria Swanson. In her Foreword to *The Twenties in Vogue* (1983), she wrote of the decade: 'Perhaps the greatest change was in woman – the world's view of her, her view of the world. There was a new spirit of freedom, a new morality … Playing Sadie Thompson in Somerset Maugham's *Rain*, I didn't just shock Hollywood by playing a prostitute who was at least an honest woman – but by producing the film myself – now that was liberation! Women

Fig.14
'Photography Comes into the Kitchen'
by Margaret Watkins
Vanity Fair, October 1921

Vanity Fair championed modernism, such as the work of Margaret Watkins – a testament to the agenda-setting nature of Crowninshield's editorship. These domestic still-life subjects caused considerable controversy as to whether such material was eligible for 'artistic treatment'.

Fig.15
'Portrait of an American Family: 1924'
by Edward Steichen
Vanity Fair, May 1924

Steichen later retitled this modernist study 'Laughing Boxes: West 86th Street, New York'. The *Vanity Fair* caption reads: 'Here we have a photograph of an American family, far more accurate, far more revealing, than any combination of faces and figures could be.'

Fig.16
'The White Door' by Charles Sheeler
Vanity Fair, April 1923

Charles Sheeler's work was much admired by Condé Nast. This study is from Sheeler's Doylestown House series of 18th-century Pennsylvanian interiors. The *Vanity Fair* caption reads: 'In this example of his camera work the painter is everywhere evident ...'

at last were pressing for equality, reacting ... to years of oppression by the so-called dominant male.'

Vanity Fair reflected the extraordinary number of women photographers active throughout this period, whose works were credited in the magazine. Its first decade featured images, among others, by the pictorialists Annie Brigman and Gertrude Käsebier, the noted American portraitists Alice Boughton and Frances Benjamin Johnston, and the theatre photographers Marcia Stein, Charlotte Fairchild and Aimée Dupont. It also promoted the artists Frida Kahlo (p.68), Malvina Hoffman and Tamara de Lempicka, and produced colour art supplements that included the works of Georgia O'Keeffe (p.69), Marie Laurencin and Elsa Jack von Reppert Bismarck. Over the next two decades this roll call of female portraitists would continue.

During the 1910s and 1920s, a number of women photographers were publishing their work in the British weeklies, and they were soon commissioned by *Vanity Fair*. Lizzie Caswall Smith, Miss Compton Collier (represented here by her 'at home' study of H.G. Wells, p.42) as well as Dorothy Wilding and Madame Yevonde all contributed work to the magazine, as did Madame

d'Ora (Dora Kallmus), who sent contributions from Vienna until the 1930s.

The British-born Florence Vandamm (1883–1966) was one of the most successful New York theatre photographers of all time, ebulliently portraying a glimpse of the Jazz Age with such images as her portrait of screen star Alice White, in a carefully concocted nightclub scene that sums up late 1920s life in New York. She had started her career as an artist before opening her first London photographic studio in 1908. Ten years later she married an American engineer, George R. Thomas, and subsequently taught him to paint. With the downturn of work in Britain they moved to the United States in 1923 and found work at the theatrical portrait business of Francis Brugière, a regular contributor to *Vanity Fair*, for whom they covered when necessary. As Brugière moved into more experimental and abstract work, they laboured day and night to establish themselves as the leading Broadway photographers, with Florence operating from the studio at West 57th Street and 'Tommy' taking the onstage cast ensembles. The works reproduced here (pp.82,85) reflect their two approaches to set-piece theatrical portrait

photography, with White in the studio and the Rasch Dancers on the stage.

The modernist work of the Canadian-born pictorialist Margaret Watkins (1884–1969) was published in 1921, an early example of household objects used as suitable subjects for fine art photography (fig.14). One of the students of Clarence H. White, who succeeded Alfred Stieglitz as the leader of American art photography, Watkins's importance lay in her ability to move from pictorialism to a modernism suitable for advertising, a path she trod with fellow White students Margaret Bourke-White and Anton Bruehl.

Emergent American women photographers of the 1920s include two who were based in Paris, Helen Pierce Breaker and Therese Bonney (1894–1978). Breaker had established her reputation as an art photographer in St Louis earlier in the decade, before moving to Paris and setting up a studio there. Her study of Ernest Hemingway wearing his cap (p.64) was one of a number taken in March 1928. Hemingway had been living in Paris from 1920, on the advice of Sherwood Anderson, and became a member of Gertrude Stein's circle. His 1926 book *The Sun Also Rises* described

Portrait of an American Family: 1924

The White Door: A Study by Charles Sheeler

the experiences of American expatriates in Europe and used as an epigraph Stein's comment that theirs was a 'lost generation'. Bonney recorded the Japanese-born artist Foujita, who had arrived in Paris in 1913 and quickly established himself as a leading figure in the artists' quarter in Montparnasse (André Kertész was to photograph Foujita in the same location in 1933 [p.86]).[9]

Modernism and Man Ray

From 1917 to 1922 De Meyer's portraits had dominated the magazine, but by 1923 he was wanting to return to Europe and was lured away to work for rival magazine *Harper's Bazaar*, with its less demanding strictures. It was a time of change and left a fortuitous gap to be filled by others, who would continue to develop an ever more modernist style.

In 1922 the first of these was the American painter-turned-photographer Man Ray (1890–1976). Born Emmanuel Radnitsky in Philadelphia, he moved with his family to New York in 1897, where he attended art classes at the Ferrer Center. Here he met European and American artists at Stieglitz's 291 Gallery. At the Armory Show, in which Frank

Crowninshield played an important role, the artist's meeting with Marcel Duchamp and Francis Picabia inspired his first Cubist painting, *Portrait of Alfred Stieglitz* (1915), by which time he had changed his name to Man Ray.

Initially his first camera was purchased to record his paintings but by 1920 he was collaborating photographically with Duchamp and followed him to Paris in 1921. It was during this year, and the next, that he became a highly committed portraitist. His first portrait to appear in *Vanity Fair* was of the Dadaist founder Tristan Tzara (June 1922), which was accompanied by the latter's article 'Some Memoirs of Dadaism', which treated *Vanity Fair*'s American readership to one of several front-row insights into contemporary French, as well as international, counter-culture.

The following month his portraits of Picasso and James Joyce made their debut. In the August issue possibly one of his greatest portraits, that of Gertrude Stein, was published (p.65). Stein is shown in her Paris studio at 27 rue de Fleurus, where she acted as friend, patron and hostess to a generation of Americans visiting Paris including Ernest Hemingway, F. Scott Fitzgerald and Sherwood Anderson.

Other works published in 1922 in *Vanity Fair* were Man Ray's portraits of the sculptor Jacques Lipchitz and Nijinsky's sister, Nijinska, in remarkable theatrical make-up designed by Mikhail Larionov for the modernist ballet *Kikimora*, devised for Diaghilev's Ballets Russes by Léonide Massine in 1916 (p.75). The inclusion of four rayographs in *Vanity Fair* the following year, alongside a profile of Man Ray's career up to that date, is considered a decisive moment in this photographer's avant-garde career.

Man Ray was based in Paris until the late 1930s. His images continued to feature in *Vanity Fair* and his last portrait – a profile study of Picasso, captioned 'Picasso – a one-man revolution in art' and 'Made in Paris by Man Ray' – appeared as a full-page reproduction in October, 1934 (p.71). Man Ray's influence on the magazine can also be seen in the work of his two pupil/assistants, which it subsequently published: Berenice Abbott, whose Paris portraits include studies of James Joyce (p.54) and Marie Laurencin; and Lee Miller, Man Ray's model and muse, who contributed portraits such as those of the writer George Slocombe and the actress Claire Luce with her Siamese cat.

The Early Steichen Years

In 1923, *Vanity Fair* declared Edward Steichen to be the greatest living portrait photographer. Within a year, publisher Condé Nast, turning De Meyer's defection into an opportunity, had appointed Steichen chief photographer of *Vanity Fair* and its fashion counterpart, *Vogue*. For the next thirteen years, Steichen was America's leading photographer of style, taste and celebrity. While his work at *Vanity Fair* embraced numerous genres, Steichen is perhaps best remembered for creating many of the icons of his age – personalities from the film world whose likenesses, in print or on screen, helped shape America's popular culture.

Edward Steichen (1879–1973), who was born in Luxembourg, had come to America in 1881.[10] He studied art and was then apprenticed as a designer in a lithographic company. He took his first photographs in 1896, working in a pictorial style, and exhibited his work in 1899, enjoying considerable success in the first decade of the twentieth century with the Photo-Secessionists. Steichen photographed the world of avant-garde theatre from as early as 1908 and, like Stieglitz, helped support and showcase

17

Fig.17
Virginia Woolf by Maurice Beck
and Helen MacGregor,
British *Vogue*, May 1926
Vanity Fair, September 1929

This photograph, which shows the
novelist wearing her mother's dress,
was later re-used in a circular
vignette in *Vanity Fair*'s September
1929 'Hall of Fame'.

Fig.18
Virginia Woolf by Maurice Beck
and Helen MacGregor
Previously unpublished

This study of Virginia Woolf survived
in a scrapbook compiled by Cecil
Beaton, who greatly admired this
bohemian photographic partnership.
Beck and MacGregor contributed
portrait and fashion photographs
to Condé Nast magazines from
1922 onwards.

modern artists engaged in this context, organizing exhibitions of their work at 291 – Matisse in 1908, Cezanne in 1910 and Brancusi in 1914.

Crowninshield was a huge admirer of Steichen's work and the magazine featured his portrait of Matisse shortly after it was reproduced in *Camera Work* (issue no.42, in 1912).

From 1909 Steichen spent much of his time on his farm at Voulangis, France, temporarily having given up photography in favour of painting. Following his divorce in 1922, however, he returned to America with the aim of pursuing new directions. Amused at *Vanity Fair*'s profile of himself as the 'greatest living portrait photographer', he offered his services. In 1923 a meeting was arranged and hard bargaining ensued. Steichen negotiated a salary of $35,000 per year[1] – a staggering amount for the time. He was to work for the magazine until its demise in 1936, and then continued for a further two years after some of *Vanity Fair*'s sections were incorporated into *Vogue*. The recruitment of Steichen gave *Vanity Fair* its photographic authority throughout the 1920s and early 1930s. In his *The History of Photography*, published in 1964, the influential curator, art historian, writer and photographer Beaumont Newhall elegantly summarized Steichen's portraits for Condé Nast's magazines as follows: 'These photographs are brilliant and forceful; they form a pictorial biography of the men of letters, actors, artists, statesmen of the 1920s and 1930s, doing for that generation what Nadar did for the mid-nineteenth century intellectual world of Paris.'

Newhall's male-oriented list of subjects was extended by Steichen to include noted sportswomen and adventuresses, such as Helen Wills Moody and Amelia Earhart; dancers, such Isadora Duncan and Martha Graham; writers, such as Dorothy Parker and Colette (p.108); and screen actresses too numerous to mention.

Although most of his portraits were specially commissioned for *Vanity Fair*, key works taken previously were made more famous by virtue of being published in the magazine. These included his full-length study of Isadora Duncan (p.66), taken on a trip to Athens in 1920, which shows her stretching upwards, perfectly framed by the Grecian columns of the Acropolis; and a photograph of Edward Gordon Craig, the theatre designer and son of Ellen Terry, taken in Paris in the same year, in which he is silhouetted in front of the massive side elevation of Notre Dame (p.67).

Steichen's portrait of the comedienne Fanny Brice in top hat and tails (p.73) marked a watershed in his early photographic style. In his autobiography Steichen noted, 'Since I did not have a studio of my own, the first portrait sittings I did for *Vanity Fair* were photographed in the studios of the New York Camera Club'. When the print of Brice was offered for sale at Sotheby's, New York (17 April 2002), the cataloguer noted, 'With its compositional dependence on rectilinear background elements, this image provides a transition from the aesthetics of Steichen's pre-war pictorial portraits to his later, more glamorizing magazine work.' In addition to his portraits, *Vanity Fair* also boldly published Steichen's more elliptical modernist works, such as a shadowgram of a brick-and-iron railing, taken from a tenement block fire exit, which he entitled, 'Portrait of an American Family: 1924' (fig.15). This can be seen as part of Crowninshield's continuing campaign to introduce modernist subject matter in photography (see also Charles Sheeler, fig.16). By favouring a purer, more

realistic form of photography Steichen effectively broke away from Stieglitz. The experience he gained during the First World War, during which he commanded the photographic division of the American Expeditionary Forces, may have played a part (pin-sharp photographic results were required for accurate mapping). Stieglitz could not accept that commercial, commissioned photography could ever be considered art, whilst Steichen felt no such scruples, if the photographer could maintain his artistic principles.

Steichen's most celebrated portrait of 1924 was of Gloria Swanson (p.96).[12] Swanson, now more associated with her *grand guignol* appearance in the 1950s film noir *Sunset Boulevard*, was in the 1920s one of the most popular and well-paid stars of the silent era. Steichen provides a vivid account of the sitting, taken in the year in which six of her films were released.[13] 'The day I made the picture, Gloria Swanson and I had had a long session, with many changes of costume and different lighting effects. At the end of the session, I took a piece of black lace veil and hung it in front of her face. She recognized the idea at once. Her eyes dilated, and her look was that of a leopardess lurking

behind leafy shrubbery, watching her prey. You don't have to explain things to a dynamic and intelligent personality like Miss Swanson. Her mind works swiftly and intuitively.'

Two of his most powerful images from 1928 feature the contrasting appeal of Louise Brooks and Greta Garbo. Brooks had risen from being a dancer in the Ziegfeld Follies to taking small comedy roles in American films, but seemed doomed, as the *Vanity Fair* caption writer wrote, to 'routine parts in program pictures'. With the headline 'the Film Actress, once of the Chorus, is now working for a German Film company', Steichen's beguiling and thoughtful study of Brooks (p.103), taken in Los Angeles, caught the moment before she left America to work with G.W. Pabst, with whom she found the perfect roles in the two films she made in Weimar Germany (*Pandora's Box* and *Diary of a Lost Girl*) and in which her legacy resides. Steichen's picture is simple and effective in portraying her timeless appeal: the crisp, asymmetrical composition, and even her pageboy haircut, seem as fresh as if taken yesterday.

Garbo's portrait (p.109) has become even more enduring, the bold close-up having emerged over time as a photographic icon. Steichen again gives an insight

into its creation, recording how he found the perfect gesture. By holding her hands to her head to hide her inappropriately styled hair, Garbo in fact created one of her most emblematic studies.

As with Brooks, who had to go to Europe to make her most significant films, so with the Chinese-American star Anna May Wong, who travelled to Europe in 1929. Her work in Germany and London raised, albeit temporarily, her status and led to her role with Marlene Dietrich in Josef von Sternberg's *Shanghai Express* (1932). Steichen's 1932 portrait of Wong (p.102) seems a photographic echo of Brancusi's sculpture *Sleeping Muse*.

Cecil Beaton and his Contemporaries

Cecil Beaton (1904–80) was another favourite, and consistent, star photographer who worked for the Condé Nast group in the 1920s. Beaton's work appeared principally in *Vogue*, *Vanity Fair*'s sister title, but he did take a number of special sittings for *Vanity Fair* as well as contributing colour drawings and caricatures of Hollywood stars. One such sitting published in 1929 featured the extraordinary Sitwells (p.62) –

the eccentric, avant-garde siblings Sacheverell, Osbert and Edith – who had helped to introduce Beaton to bohemia and the provocative new art scene.[14]

The Sitwells had been launched photographically in the pages of British *Vogue*, then under the editorship of Dorothy Todd, through the photographs of Maurice Beck (1887–1960) and Helen MacGregor. This partnership between the two photographers and the editor had made them the *de facto* official photographers to the avant-garde literary set and denizens of Bloomsbury. Their images of the Sitwells appeared in *Vanity Fair* in 1924, followed by their portraits of T.S. Eliot, Somerset Maugham and the fabulously garbed Léonide Massine in costume for *Le Carnaval* (p.74). Their medallion portrait of Rebecca West (p.60), one of the most significant feminist authors of the twentieth century and for many years the secret mistress of H.G. Wells, and the romantic images of Virginia Woolf (figs 17, 18; p.61), wearing her mother's long-sleeved dress,[15] are some of the very few surviving prints by this photographic partnership. West was profiled in *Vanity Fair*'s 'Hall of Fame' during a lecture tour of America in 1924. 'She is politically

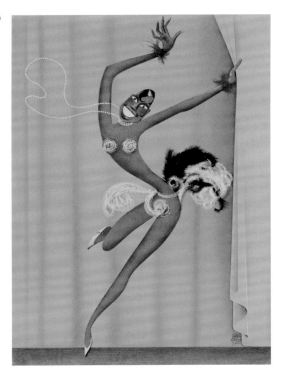

19

one of the most active women in Europe … has contributed support at once wise and intrepid to the cause of female suffrage in England … she remains young, beautiful, brilliant, genuine, and feminine'. Woolf sat twice for Beck and MacGregor in 1924 and 1925 at their exotically decorated studio at 4 Marylebone Mews, which she recorded in her diary.

Averse to sitting for professional photographers, Woolf had turned down several requests from Beaton to take her portrait. When Beaton's first book of drawings, photographs and essays was published as *The Book of Beauty* (1930), Woolf was horrified to find herself included, for Beaton had re-interpreted the classic Beck and MacGregor images as line drawings. (More than eighty years later Annie Leibovitz would continue to add to the mythical iconography of Virginia Woolf by photographing Nicole Kidman, who played the writer in the film *The Hours*, posed in the Charleston farmhouse that was the home of Woolf's sister Vanessa Bell and a Bloomsbury shrine [see p.192].)

Beaton was signed to *Vogue* from 1926 as an illustrator, caricaturist, diarist, portrait and fashion photographer. Though Beck and MacGregor were Beaton's predecessors on *Vogue*,

these photographers overlapped with each other as rival image-makers. Despite this, Beck and MacGregor were generous with their advice to the up-and-coming photographer, who was inspired by their approach (an emphasis on ambience whether bohemian or oriental) and techniques (use of silver paper), which he keenly adopted and adapted. Beaton's society contacts, his visits to Hollywood, and his obsession and romance with Garbo provided numerous pictures for *Vanity Fair* including notable studies of Gary Cooper, Loretta Young, Merle Oberon and Sybil Thorndike. Beaton could be relied upon to create the unusual, utilizing a highly imaginative approach and preferring – against Nast's wishes – to work with a small-format camera rather than the standard 10 x 8in studio model, which, it was felt, produced the best quality work and almost to the same size as the reproductions in the magazine.

American Modernists and Charles Sheeler

Early in 1926 Steichen asked his friend the modernist painter and photographer Charles Sheeler (1883–1965) to join him on the staff at *Vanity Fair*. Sheeler had

been a student at Pennsylvania Academy of Fine Arts, studying under William Merritt Chase. He had shown six paintings at the Armory Show and also started taking photographs around that time, alternating his work in both media. *Vanity Fair* had heralded his artistic credentials early on, reproducing his photograph of a Brancusi sculpture in 1917, his still life of leaves in 1920, and one of his studies of the Park Row skyscraper building, captioned 'Cubist Architecture of New York', in 1921. Two years later, as part of Crowninshield's continuing campaign to introduce modernist subject matter in photography, the magazine reproduced as a full-page plate one of his Doylestown house images (fig.16). Captioned 'The White Door', it shows a haunting open door and staircase.

Between April 1926 and June 1929, when he left *Vanity Fair* to travel to Europe where he took an important series of photographs of Chartres Cathedral, Sheeler contributed sixty portraits of variable quality of celebrities of the day,[16] but he found many of the sittings irksome, preferring the industrial scenes and cityscapes for which he is best known to human still lifes. His best portraits for the magazine included those of Theodore Dreiser (July 1926),

Norma Shearer and the boxer George Carpentier, whilst his acknowledged masterpiece is of the British-born Aldous Huxley (p.56), a regular *Vanity Fair* contributor who was visiting America and who later settled in California in 1937. Huxley had already established a reputation with his first two novels *Crome Yellow* (1921) and *Antic Hay* (1923), based on his experiences of the First World War and of Bloomsbury and Garsington, and then went on to produce his masterpiece *Brave New World* (1932), based partly on his experiences of 'Americanization' throughout the world at this time. Sheeler's three-quarter-length portrait of Huxley is a perfect combination of contrasting but subtle lighting, strong graphic composition and sympathetically portrayed subject suggesting thoughtfulness and intelligence.

Modernism in Europe: George Hoyningen-Huene

Sheeler's travels to Europe coincided with the *Film und Foto* show in Stuttgart, where he was one of ten American photographers represented, including Berenice Abbott, Edward Weston, Steichen and Imogen Cunningham, all of whom contributed at some point to *Vanity Fair*. In the European section of this landmark exhibition, photography's equivalent of the Armory Show, were works by Baron George Hoyningen-Huene (1900–1968), who had been recruited to the magazine in 1927.

Sometimes known as the 'Baltic Baron', Huene was born in St Petersburg, grew up in Eastern Europe and was educated in England following the Russian Revolution. Based in Paris, his entry into photography came via his collaboration with Man Ray, in 1924, on a fashion photography portfolio, later sold to a New England department store. This gained him illustration work for French *Vogue*. He also acted as photographic assistant to American photographer Alexander O'Neill. When Huene took his first portrait for *Vanity Fair* of Igor Stravinsky (p.70) in 1927, Huene had already been working for *Vogue* as a fashion photographer for a year, based primarily in *Vogue*'s Paris studio. His astonishing portrait of Josephine Baker (p.79), the American dancer who first found fame in Paris in *La Revue Nègre*, was included in the *Film und Foto* show but not deemed suitable at the time for *Vanity Fair*; however, three other portraits of her did appear in other issues (see also figs 20, 21).[17] The magazine's interest in Baker also extended to commissioning Paolo Garretto's exuberant, feathered and naked colour caricature (fig.19), which appeared in the last issue of the jazz era magazine.

Huene made two trips to America, during which he visited New York and Hollywood: the first in 1929 and the second in 1934, when he was at the artistic peak of his career. *Vanity Fair* sent him to Hollywood to make a comprehensive portfolio that included pictures of Gary Cooper (p.98), Cary Grant (p.113) and Katharine Hepburn, barelegged and evocatively posed in a high-backed wicker chair, as well as James Cagney and director Ernst Lubitsch.

Huene, like De Meyer, was prone to dramatic moods and shortly thereafter, due to a contract dispute, he severed his connections with Nast and moved to the long-term rival magazine *Harper's Bazaar*. He proved a great influence on Horst P. Horst, whom he had met in 1930, at first using him as a fashion model, and also on Irving Penn, Richard Avedon and others, whose work would appear fifty years later in the new incarnation of *Vanity Fair*.

Berlin – London – New York

In 1929, to accompany a Paul Morand review, the magazine used quirky scraperboard drawings by a 19-year-old artist who had been dubbed the 'Marie Laurencin of Berlin', one Elsa Jack von Reppert Bismarck. She remained a favourite with the magazine and Rolf Mahrenholz's photograph of her (p.87) conveys the excitement of youthful artistic creativity, anticipating the look of a much later twentieth-century practitioner such as Cindy Sherman.[18] Mahrenholz (1902–1991) was one of a large number of German artists and photographers who were to leave their country in the wake of Hitler's rise to power and resettle in the West. Born in Koenigsberg, East Prussia he arrived in Berlin in 1921, aged 19, to learn photography in an established portrait studio and quickly made a reputation for himself, particularly for a series of portraits of leading Danish film star Asta Nielsen. He married a Jewish sculptor, Paminma Liebert, in 1929, but with the foreboding political climate, left Germany and made a career in London.

Works supplied to the magazine by German studio photographers also included a number of images from Bieber of Berlin. The firm

George Grosz
German satirist

Fig.22
George Grosz by Horst P. Horst
Vanity Fair, November 1933

Fig.23
King Fuad of Egypt and
German president
Paul von Hindenburg by
Dr Erich Salomon, 1931
Detail published in
Vanity Fair, December 1932

To mark King Fuad's visit to
Germany, a special performance
of *Der Rosenkavalier*, directed
by Richard Strauss, was produced
at the State Opera in Berlin.
This photograph was taken during
the intermission, a 'candid
camera study'.

had been founded in nineteenth-century Hamburg by Emilie Bieber, who passed the business on to her nephew Leonard Bieber, who moved the photographic business to Berlin. In turn his son Auguste Emil Julius Bieber took over the studio; he fled Germany in 1933 when Adolf Hitler was elected chancellor and took the studio to Cape Town, South Africa and a new beginning.

The work of George Grosz (1892–1959), one of the most extreme of twentieth-century caricaturists, was represented in several issues of *Vanity Fair*, ranging from photomontages to colour reproductions of his drawings of the underbelly of life. He left Germany to settle in New York in 1933 and was benignly portrayed by Horst, seated in full-frontal pose with his notebook open and his pipe in his mouth (fig.22). The image supplied by the Bieber studio in Berlin, although not run by the magazine at the time, was safely stored in the Condé Nast Archive and illustrates Grosz more tellingly. Posed in profile against his painting *Self-portrait with Model* from 1928 (p.89), the image immediately conjures up the man and his work. This portrait has subsequently taken on even greater interest. Much of Grosz's work was dubbed

as decadent and destroyed by the Nazis but this painting, by a circuitous route, was donated in 1954 to New York's Museum of Modern Art. Other photographs by Bieber, published in *Vanity Fair*, include a study of Albert Einstein, which was run full-page as the frontispiece to the June 1929 issue.

Photojournalism: A New Genre

The late 1920s saw the development of a new kind of photography: photojournalism. In Paris in the 1920s James Abbe, who had previously worked with stars on the New York stage and on the sets of the films of D.W. Griffith, began to take and make the picture stories that were featured in 'new look' German magazines such as *Biz*, *Die Dame* and *Munich Illustrierte Zeitung* as well as a French equivalent, *Vu*, created by Lucien Vogel. On visits to Germany between 1931 and 1933 he charted the rise of Adolf Hitler and Nazi Germany. His portraits of Hitler, Goebbels and Goering made a chilling contribution to the December 1933 issue of *Vanity Fair*.

Other photographers emerged as stars while working

for these picture magazines, including the two Hungarian-born photographers previously mentioned: André Kertész (1894–1985), who arrived in Paris in 1925, and Martin Munkacsi (1896–1963). Munkacsi left a successful career operating a studio in Budapest to begin a three-year contract with the German publishing house Ullstein in Berlin in 1928. He moved to America in 1934 and became *Harper's Bazaar*'s top fashion photographer, eventually inspiring the photographic careers of both Henri Cartier-Bresson and Richard Avedon.

Munkacsi's study of Leni Riefenstahl on skis may be from her 1929 film the *White Hell of Pitz Palu*, one of her series of 'Mountain' films, and was published on the cover of *Berlin Illustrierte Zeitung* for 11 January 1931 (p.81). Riefenstahl turned from acting to directing, and in 1936 made the controversial masterpiece *Triumph of the Will*, which glorified Hitler and the Nuremberg rallies, as well as the official film of the Berlin Olympics. Reporting on these controversial Games, *Time* magazine featured Riefenstahl on the cover of its February 1936 edition, using Munkacsi's iconic image, which had appeared two years earlier in *Vanity Fair*.

The rise of the small-format and easily concealable Ermanox camera provided the opportunity for Dr Erich Salomon (1886–1944) to invent a new genre, that of 'candid' photography. Salomon got his first scoop when he smuggled a camera into a courtroom during a murder trial in 1928. Smartly dressed, cultivated, and with a confident manner, Salomon gained entry to political events and discussions barred to other photographers.

Originally working for the publicity department of the Ullstein press in Berlin, he graduated to freelance work for the London *Graphic* and then travelled to America to work for the newly launched *Fortune* magazine. He also contributed picture stories to four issues of *Vanity Fair*, ranging from pro-Prohibition meetings to American senators caught unawares and asleep in Congress ('Wide awake Congress') to Bruno Walter conducting. In the year these appeared Salomon fled Germany for the Netherlands but was subsequently betrayed and died in Auschwitz. His 1931 study of President Hindenburg and King Fuad of Egypt (fig.23), taken at the Berlin opera house, is a testament to Salomon's resourcefulness at getting inside access to the powerful.

The Wall Street Crash

The lavish number of advertising pages that helped to underwrite *Vanity Fair* stayed high through the 'Roaring Twenties'. In fact some of the magazine's best issues came out in 1929. But then, in October, the New York stock market crashed. Nast suffered severely when his stock fell from a high of $93 to just $4.50. The main effect of this economic disaster on the magazine was a reduction in the scale of advertising, from fifty pages before the crash to about twenty and then just five as the decade progressed. New directors in 1932 replaced the literary contributions with more serious political content and the covers changed from decorative designs to illustrations featuring Roosevelt, Hitler and other global political figures. Most of the picture content, however, remained more or less untouched, with Steichen's work maintaining its excellence.

Nast's plans to publish in colour and to introduce better quality printing by acquiring new presses went ahead. His meticulous balance sheets and costings show that everything was closely analysed and give an intriguing insight into the sums involved in producing a luxury magazine. It was an expensive gamble.

The Later Steichen Years

In the 1930s, Hollywood was still America's foremost entertainment industry, its stars the film world's most potent and alluring product. The Depression of the 1930s saw Americans escaping to the world of the cinema, a refuge from the stark realities of daily life.

More than mere reflections of a single personality, Steichen's portraits were cultural manifestations of the American public's consuming fascination with celebrity and fame. His close-up study of Paul Robeson (p.106), in costume for the filming of the Eugene O'Neill play *The Emperor Jones* (1933), powerfully conveys the actor's outsize presence. Playing the stage role in London in the 1920s had enhanced Robeson's early career and the later film made him, for a time, a cinematic figure as well.[19] In contrast, Steichen created the quintessential portrait of an idealized, immaculately good-mannered and perfectly turned-out English gentleman in his study of the British actor Leslie Howard (p.107), who would later enjoy considerably greater transatlantic exposure playing Ashley Wilkes in *Gone with the Wind* (1939). He died prematurely, shot down by the Nazis in the Second World War

whilst reportedly returning from a secret mission in Lisbon.

Fellow Briton Charles Laughton was photographed for the magazine in between three of his major film roles (p.101). By showing Laughton half-turning his head, and seated in a simple wicker chair with his hands crossed under his chin, Steichen created a guileless and sympathetic study that probes beneath the skin of the actor's complex nature and many guises.[20]

Two authors of sophistication and wit were captured by Steichen in the early 1930s: Noel Coward (p.78) and Dorothy Parker. Coward was an ideal subject for *Vanity Fair*, exuding nonchalance, style, smartness and wit. Coward made his first exploratory trips to New York, seeking to make his mark, in 1921. Crowninshield's talent spotting made the magazine the first recipient in America of a Coward contribution. Within the genre of Art Deco photography, Steichen's portraits of Coward as a lean figurine, chiselled in dark shadow, is an obvious masterpiece. Although Parker had sold her first poem to *Vanity Fair* in 1917, her first editorial job was with *Vogue*. Here she was spotted by Crowninshield, who lured her, like many other talents, across to his magazine two years later. Whilst regular theatre critic P.G. Wodehouse was on

24

Fig.24
Ethel Waters by Bruehl and Bourges
Vanity Fair, January 1934

Ethel Waters was celebrated for her performances on stage, screen, radio and television. Her Broadway shows included *As Thousands Cheer* (1933). *Vanity Fair* described how the theatre came alive when she stepped out on stage 'with a gentle wriggle of the hips and a grin as radiant as Christmas'.

Fig.25
Billy Rose's Music Hall by Bruehl and Bourges
Vanity Fair, December 1934

The nightly line-up of small-time vaudeville acts at Billy Rose's Music Hall on Broadway was 'one of the biggest sensations Manhattan show business had seen'. It included Irish Minstrels, the Swiss Bell Ringer, the Fat Girls, the Fire-eater, the Strong Woman and Willie, the trained seal.

vacation, Parker was deputised with great success. However, when her biting critiques became too personal, and her wayward work habits became too much for Crowninshield's tastes, she found herself dismissed from the staff in 1920. Robert Benchley and Robert Sherwood, who with Parker had initiated the legendary Algonquin Round Table literary lunches, both resigned in sympathy. Parker's career path, however, was established and she soon went on to write for *The New Yorker*. At the time of Steichen's portrait of her, dated 1932, she was the subject of a play by George Oppenheimer, *Here Today*.[21]

Colour in the 1930s

Although Steichen was the first photographer to have a colour portrait in *Vanity Fair* (March 1931), it was Anton Bruehl's colour work for the magazine that was the most sustained and innovative. An Australian émigré, Bruehl (1900–1983) arrived in New York from Melbourne, having trained as an electrical engineer. Through his interest in photography he met and trained under Clarence H. White, later taking over his school when White died in 1925. But in 1927 he set up a studio with his brother

Martin and teamed up with Fernand Bourges, a photo-technician, and some of Condé Nast's engravers to invent a colour photography process for use in its magazines. The process was complicated: 'one exposure required at least 300 flashbulbs' and 'three black-and-white filtered negatives, each sensitive to different colors'. The expense and trouble meant that in the depths of the Depression, Bruehl and Bourges had 'a virtual monopoly on color photography', at least until Kodachrome film was invented in 1935.

Bruehl's portfolio of work was shown extensively in *Vanity Fair*. From 1934 to 1936 the magazine published sensational studies of Ethel Waters in the musical *As Thousands Cheer* (fig.24), Helen Menken as Queen Elizabeth and Helen Hayes as Mary, Queen of Scots in a scene from Maxwell Anderson's play *Mary of Scotland* (April 1934), the dancer Toumanova in the ballet *Petrouschka* (May 1934), an exhausted boxer sitting in his ringside corner, entitled 'The Last Round' (June 1934), a group photograph of Clifton Webb, Jimmy Savo and Irene Dunne, which was used as the magazine's cover (see fig.7) and an elaborate tableau entitled 'Parade of the

old-timers at Billy Rose's Music Hall' (fig.25). These images show how far the use of colour had developed since Steichen's early colour portraits, such as the delicate flower-strewn study of Lillian Gish, fig.26.

In 1935 the first feature film photographed entirely in three-strip Technicolor, appropriately an historical adaptation of William Makepeace Thackeray's *Vanity Fair* with Miriam Hopkins as Becky Sharp, was celebrated by the magazine. By this time, however, with the introduction of small-format cameras for reportage photography, Bruehl's colour compositions were beginning to look old-fashioned.

Steichen, who was responsible for bringing colour photography to *Vanity Fair*, now seized with enthusiasm the opportunity of working with the new format cameras and 35mm Kodachrome film. He followed the lead of European immigrant photographers such as Remie Lohse, whose reportage images of theatre dressing-room scenes and documentary shots of holidaymakers on Coney Island were being featured in the magazine. Steichen's adventurous colour photograph of the Radio City Musical Dancers, captured in mid-air with a high speed camera,

was a technical triumph and his startling snap shots of ballet dancers, which appeared over a double-page spread of the October 1935 issue, anticipated by many years the action realism that was to become part of the language of fashion photography and can be seen at its best in Patrick Demarchelier's study of Natalia Vodianova (p.224) and Norman Jean Roy's Hilary Swank (p.227).

Women Photographers in the 1930s

The 1930s were years of great creativity in the photographic arts and saw the emergence of still more artistic talent. From the fringes of London's bohemia and the avant-garde came Barbara Ker-Seymer (1905–93), who collaborated with Surrealist John Banting. *Vanity Fair* published her studies of the painter Paul Nash and of Richard Hughes, the celebrated author of *High Wind in Jamaica*. From American high society, Baroness Tony Von Horn (1899–1970) made a considerable impact with her portraits of Albert Einstein, Gloria Swanson, and Hope Williams and Beatrice Lillie, whose mirror-image portrait (p.105)

plays on the title of the George Bernard Shaw play they were promoting, *Too True To Be Good*.

Margaret Bourke-White and Louise Dahl-Wolfe were two stars of the future, whose careers were associated with other magazines but whose talents were spotted by *Vanity Fair* early on. At the height of the Depression Dahl-Wolfe's moving portrait captioned 'The Smoky Mountaineer' (p.95), made a strong impact when it appeared in the November 1933 issue. Dahl-Wolfe (1895–1989) was raised in San Francisco, where she witnessed the 1906 earthquake. She studied at what became the San Francisco Art Institute and was greatly inspired by Diaghilev's Ballets Russes when it came to the city. She decided to become a photographer after a friend introduced her to Annie Brigman, whose outdoor nudes taken in the Sierra Nevada mountains and at Point Lobos she tried to imitate with her group of female friends. Dahl-Wolfe knew of these works having seen them in a special issue of Stieglitz's *Camera Work* and in *Vanity Fair*, to which as an art student she regularly subscribed.

Dahl-Wolfe's 'The Smoky Mountaineer' was a study of one of her neighbours, Mrs Ramsey, whom she met while spending

the summer of 1931 in the Ozarks. Mrs Ramsey lived in a log cabin, without electricity, in the poor rural town of Gatlinburg, Tennessee. Dahl-Wolfe was there taking photographs with her Rolleiflex camera whilst her husband, the artist Mike Wolfe, concentrated on his painting. Crowninshield greatly admired Dahl-Wolfe's work but a series of mishaps, and her unwillingness to take studio portraits of celebrities, led to her working primarily as a fashion photographer for *Harper's Bazaar*.

The Last Issue

An announcement went out in the February 1936 issue of *Vanity Fair* stating that the magazine would be merged with *Vogue* the following month. *Vanity Fair* was, in part, an economic victim of the Depression, but was also up-ended by its editorial outlook: a glib, sophisticated and high-minded periodical during a period of global upheaval. What is more, it faced competition on the newsstand. New to the field were magazines such as *Fortune*, the business title that began in 1930, and *Esquire*, founded in 1933 and aimed at the male readership on which much of *Vanity Fair*'s

advertising had depended. The periodical that had once promised to 'ignite a dinner party at fifty yards' seemed no longer in synch with the stormy times.

Yet '*Vanity Fair* was a pioneer in so many areas that it can be said to be a significant benchmark of American culture,' noted social historian Cleveland Amory. 'Indeed, it was as accurate a social barometer of its time as exists.'

And to the end the quality of its photography never wavered. Featured in the last two issues were colour photographs by Bruehl and Bourges of June Knight singing 'Begin the Beguine' and their acknowledged masterwork of a red-haired, red-lipped Marlene Dietrich in *Desire* (fig.27); and Lusha Nelson's now-lost photographs of Gypsy Rose Lee, which appeared alongside a study of Peter Lorre (p.115), made during the filming of *Crime and Punishment* – one of those memorable images that act as a kind of watershed in the history of the medium. Crowninshield moved over to *Vogue* and preserved some of *Vanity Fair*'s features within the older magazine. But it would be a long and patient wait – nearly fifty years – until the magazine could be rightfully restored to its present-day topic-setting, news-breaking incarnation.

26

Fig.26
Lillian Gish by Edward Steichen
Vanity Fair, December 1932

Fig.27
Marlene Dietrich by
Bruehl and Bourges
Vanity Fair, January 1936

Notes

1 See Caroline Seebohm, *The Man Who Was Vogue, The Life and Times of Condé Nast*, New York: Viking Press, 1982, for biographies of Nast and Crowninshield. With further information on Crowninshield in Geoffrey T. Hellman's two-part profile in *The New Yorker*, 19 and 26 September 1942.

2 This name graced a number of magazines. In America it was the title of a short-lived New York-based weekly humorous magazine that appeared between 1859 and 1863. In the United Kingdom, *Vanity Fair* was an elaborate illustrated British weekly that chronicled Victorian and Edwardian society from 1868 to 1914; a publication most notable for its witty prose and caricatures. The American title that Nast acquired began as a small-format monthly, which was launched in 1890 and gradually evolved, through various changes of ownership and redesign, into a weekly periodical under the editorship of Edward Everett Pigeon. It appeared in the 1910s as '*Vanity Fair* – the weekly Theatre Magazine' with a boast in the September 1911 issue that it reached 'the vast Luxury-loving, money-spending multitude everywhere'.

3 Whilst the *Dress* part of the magazine title was dropped, male fashion-related features continued to play an important part, appealing not only to male readers but also to relevant advertisers of motorcars and other trappings of a good life.

4 The caricaturists ranged from the American Thomas Nast to the Italian Carlo Pellegrini

(working first as 'Singe', then as 'Ape') and the British Sir Leslie Ward (working as 'Spy').

5 The National Portrait Gallery recently acquired the original drawing for the first in the series – a caricature of Benjamin Disraeli from 1869 by Carlo Pellegrini. The Gallery now holds 355 original drawings, which provided the basis of some 2,358 lithographs published in *Vanity Fair* between 1868 and 1914.

6 Roy T. Matthews and Peter Mellini, *In Vanity Fair*, London: Scolar Press, 1982.

7 Hoppé produced one of the most prestigious books in the Orbis Terrarum series, namely 'Amerika' or 'Romantic America' (1927), which was republished in 2007.

8 Pickford starred in David Belasco's production of *A Good Little Devil*, in which Lillian Gish also had a small role. Pickford was paid $175 per week but when she signed to Zukor's Famous Players later that year her salary rose to $500 per week.

9 In the 1930s, Rosa Klein, the wife of André Kertész, was working under the name of Rogi André. Her photographs of Picasso, Braque and Derain were reproduced full page in *Vanity Fair*.

10 Steichen was born Edouard Steichen, later changing his name to Edward after emigrating with his family to the United States.

11 In addition, most of the pictures he supplied, which were taken either in the magazine's studios or on annual trips to Hollywood or other locations, were costed at either $270 or $376.78 per portrait, with usually at least three or four in any monthly issue.

12 This has since become the mostly highly prized Steichen work at auction, selling at Phillips de Pury & Co, New York for $540,000 in their sale on 24 April 2007.

13 The photograph was not reproduced until 1928, to accompany publicity about her appearance in *Sadie Thompson*, one of the filmed versions of Somerset Maugham's classic story *Rain*, in which she starred opposite Lionel Barrymore. For this role she was nominated for an Academy Award as Best Actress.

14 Beaton's Sitwell study, which showed the three siblings from above, lying in a circular arrangement, was redolent of the unusual angles and perspectives of the 'New Photography' movement that was celebrated at the famous Stuttgart *Film und Foto* exhibition in 1929.

15 See Lisa Tickner, 'Mediating Generation: The Mother-Daughter Plot', in *Women Artists at the Millennium*, edited by Carol Armstrong and Catherine De Zegher, Cambridge, Mass: MIT Press, 2006.

16 He also contributed ninety works to *Vogue*. For a fuller account of Sheeler's work published in *Vanity Fair* see Theodore E. Stebbins, Jr and Norman Keyes, Jr, *Charles Sheeler: The Photographs*, Boston: Little, Brown, 1987.

17 *Vanity Fair*, February 1931 issue, p.46: 'the dark star of Harlem continues to be the bright star of Paris, in a new revue at the Casino de Paris'; and October 1934 issue, p.34.

18 Elsa von Weden, something of a child prodigy, began drawing at the age of 3, and at 17 married Jorg von Reppert

Bismarck, the great-grandson of Otto von Bismarck's first cousin. Inspired by her resemblance to child filmstar Jackie Coogan, her husband nicknamed her 'Jack', a name with which she signed her paintings. She was dubbed the 'Marie Laurencin of Berlin', and *Vanity Fair* promoted her career by publishing her scenes of Berlin nightlife. Her work was again published on the occasion of her first trip to New York in 1931 and the magazine later ran colour reproductions of her portraits of Lillian Gish and Tilly Losch.

19 One of the many things *Vanity Fair* achieved in advance of other magazines was to 'give due recognition to Negro personalities and artists ... a 1925 photograph of Florence Mills, the girl who immortalized the still popular "Bye-bye Blackbird"; a Steichen photograph of the all-Negro play *Green Pastures* which won the 1930 Pulitzer Prize; and pictures of Paul Robeson as Emperor Jones, of Ethel Waters in *As Thousands Cheer* (1934) and of Joe Louis, Louis Armstrong and Jesse Owens as they appeared in 1935' (Cleveland Amory and Frederic Bradlee, *Vanity Fair: A Cavalcade of the 1920s and 1930s*, New York: Viking Press, 1960). Owens was to win four gold medals at the Berlin Olympics in 1936 (p.111).

20 Laughton made three key films in 1935: *Mutiny on the Bounty*, in which he played Captain Bligh, *Les Misérables*, in which he played Inspector Javert, and *Ruggles of Red Gap*, in which he played Ruggles.

21 The role of Dorothy Parker was played by Ruth Gordon.

Sources

See also Select Bibliography, p.246.

Steven Bach, *Leni: The Life and Work of Leni Riefenstahl*, London: Little, Brown, 2007; New York: Knopf, 2007.

Louise Dahl-Wolfe, *A Photographer's Scrapbook*, Preface by Frances McFadden, London: Quartet Books, London, 1984.

F.C. Gundlach (ed.), *Martin Munkacsi*, texts and research by Klaus Honnef and Enno Kaufhold, foreword by Richard Avedon, London: Thames and Hudson, 2006.

E.O. Hoppé, *Romantic America: Picturesque United States*, New York: B. Westermann & Co, 1927.

Hank O'Neal, *Berenice Abbott, Sixty Years of Photography*, London: Thames and Hudson, 1982.

Terence Pepper, *Camera Portraits by E.O. Hoppé*, London: National Portrait Gallery, 1978.

——, *The Lure of the Limelight: James Abbe, Photographer of Cinema and Stage*, exh. cat., London: National Portrait Gallery, 1995.

——, *James Abbe Photographer*, expanded edition, foreword by Brooks Johnson, Norfolk, Virginia: Chrysler Museum of Art, 2000.

——, *Beaton Portraits*, London: National Portrait Gallery, 2004.

Terence Pepper and Robin Muir, *Horst Portraits: Paris, London, New York*, London: National Portrait Gallery, 2001.

Philip Prodger, *E.O. Hoppé's Amerika: Modernist Photographs from the 1920s*, New York: W.W. Norton, 2007.

Edward Steichen, *A Life in Photography*, London: W.H. Allen, in collaboration with the Museum of Modern Art, New York, 1963; New York: Chanticleer Press, 1963.

VANITY FAIR PORTRAITS 1913-36
THE PLATES

Vaslav Nijinsky
by Baron De Meyer 1911 (published in *Vanity Fair* 1916)

H.G. Wells
by Compton Collier 1916

Irving Berlin
by Brown Brothers 1914

William Orpen
by Malcolm Arbuthnot 1916

Willa Cather
by E.O. Hoppé 1921

George Arliss
by Baron De Meyer 1918

Charlie Chaplin
by Baron De Meyer 1920

Lillian and Dorothy Gish
by James Abbe 1921

Adele Astaire and Fred Astaire
by James Abbe 1926

Russian Masters
L–R: Ivan Moskvin, Constantin Stanislavski, Feodor Chaliapin (seated), Vassily Katchaloff, Savely Sorine
by Arnold Genthe 1923

Les Six
L-R: Germaine Tailleferre, Francis Poulenc, Arthur Honegger, Darius Milhaud, Jean Cocteau (sitting in for Louis Durey), Georges Auric
by Isabey 1921

James Joyce
by Berenice Abbott 1926

George Bernard Shaw
by Malcolm Arbuthnot 1920

Aldous Huxley
by Charles Sheeler 1926

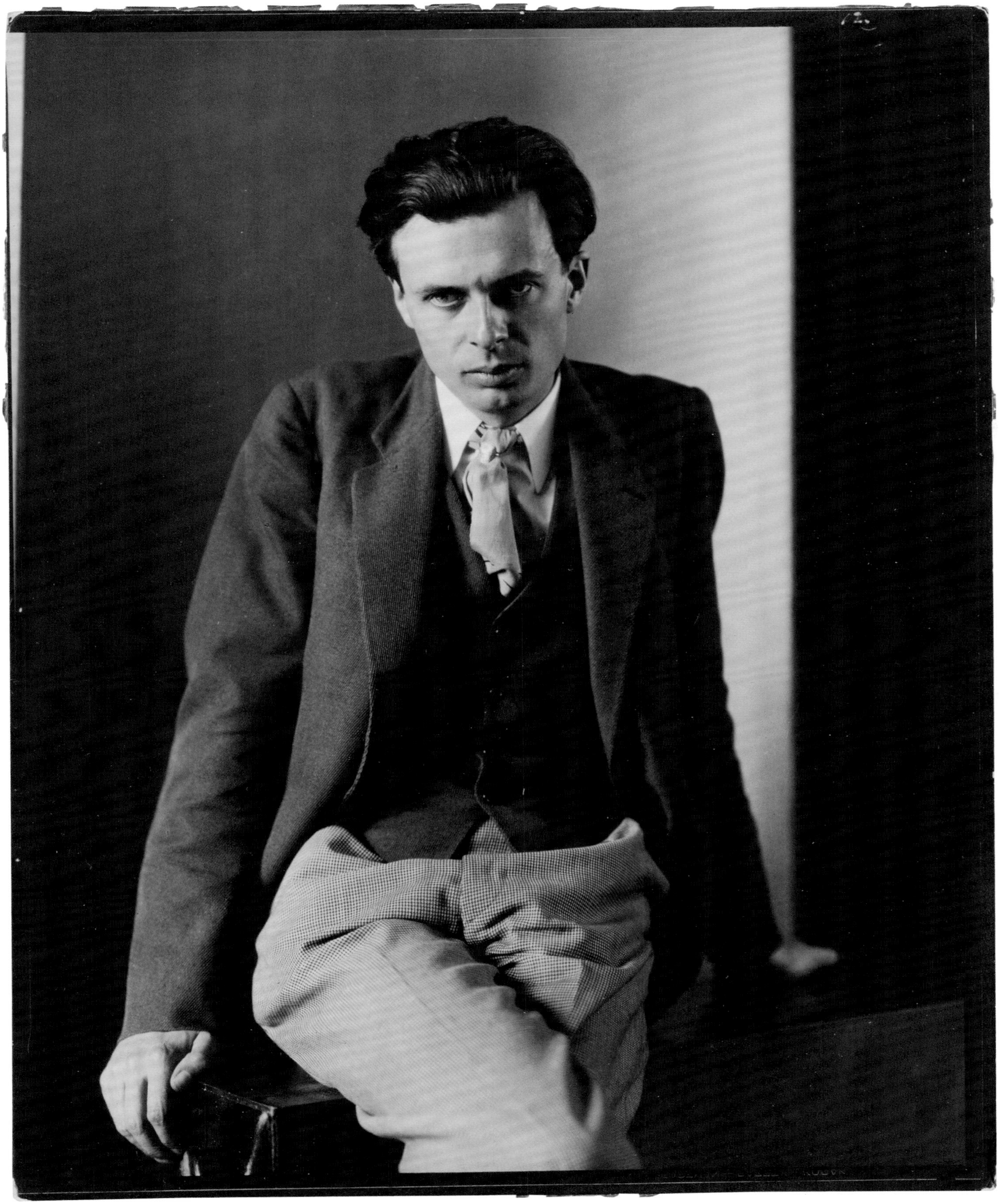

Agnes De Mille
by Nickolas Muray 1928

Rebecca West
by Maurice Beck and Helen MacGregor 1924

Virginia Woolf
by Maurice Beck and Helen MacGregor 1924

Ernest Hemingway
by Helen Pierce Breaker 1928

Isadora Duncan
by Edward Steichen 1920

Frida Kahlo and Diego Rivera
by Peter A. Juley 1931

Igor Stravinsky
by George Hoyningen-Huene 1927

Pablo Picasso
by Man Ray 1932

W.C. Fields
by Edward Steichen 1925

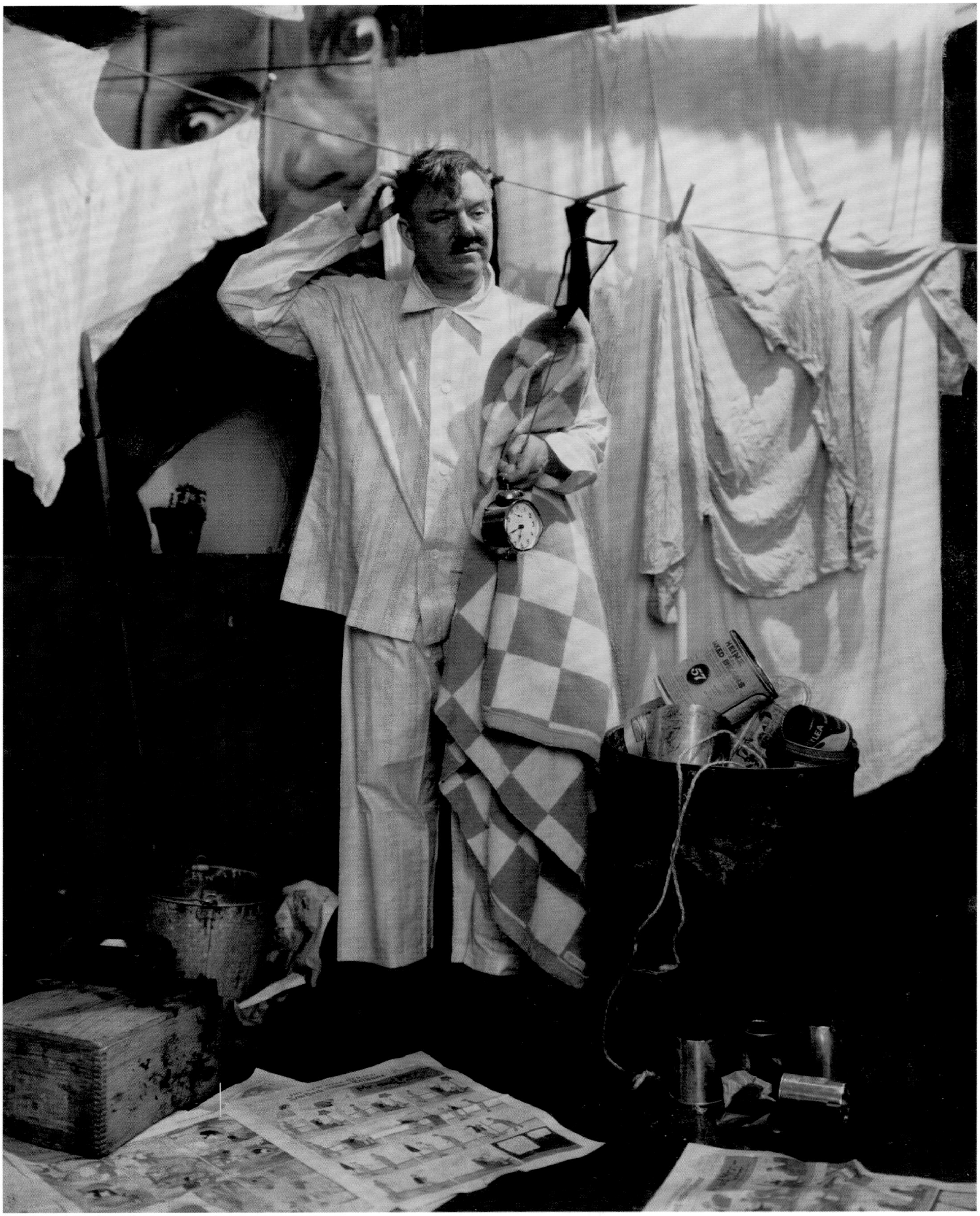

Léonide Massine
by Maurice Beck and Helen MacGregor 1923

Douglas Fairbanks, Jr and Joan Crawford
by Nickolas Muray 1929

Noel Coward, New York
by Edward Steichen 1932

Amelia Earhart
by Max Peter Haas 1933

Albertina Rasch Dancers
by Florence Vandamm 1927

Bill 'Bojangles' Robinson
by George Hurrell 1935

Elsa Jack von Reppert Bismarck
by Rolf Mahrenholz 1931

Jean Cocteau
by Cecil Beaton 1934

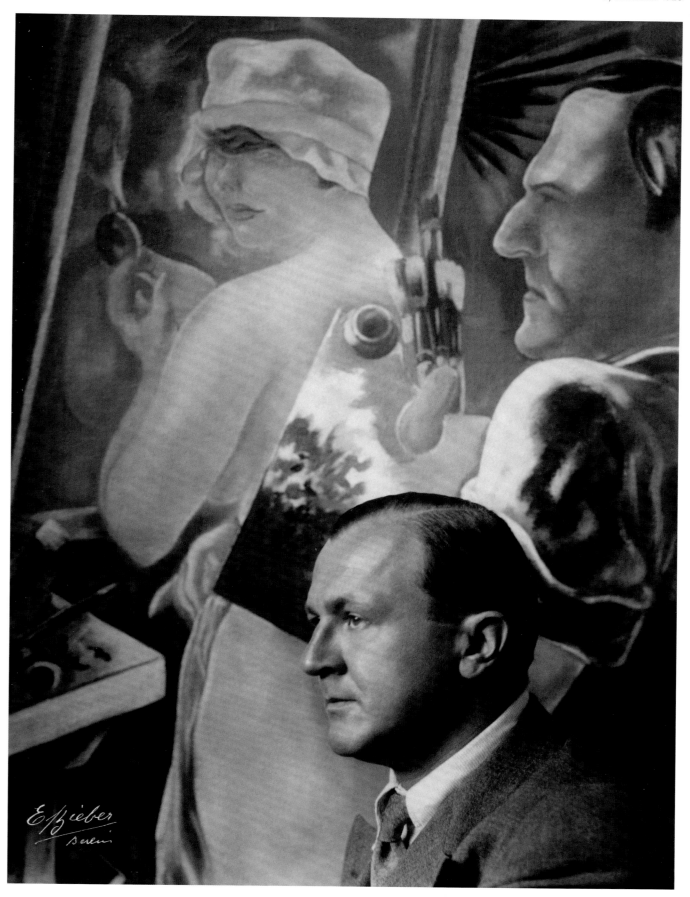

Albert Einstein
by Martin Höhlig 1923

Martha Graham
by Imogen Cunningham 1931

Ernst Lubitsch
by Imogen Cunningham 1932

Claude Monet
by Nickolas Muray 1926

The Smoky Mountaineer (Mrs Ramsey, Tennessee)
by Louise Dahl-Wolfe 1931

Gary Cooper
by George Hoyningen-Huene 1934

Sergei Eisenstein
by Barre 1930

Anna May Wong
by Edward Steichen 1930

Louise Brooks — Hollywood — Aug — 1928 — NO. 3.

Louis Armstrong
by Anton Bruehl 1935

Babe Ruth
by Nickolas Muray c.1930

Jean Harlow
by George Hurrell 1934

Ethel Merman
by Anton Bruehl and Fernand Bourges 1933

VANITY FAIR PORTRAITS 1983-2008

GETTING YOUR OWN PHOTO SHOOT IN VANITY FAIR HAS BECOME THE PREMIER ACHIEVEMENT IN OUR CELEBRITY-MAD CULTURE.

MAUREEN DOWD, *THE NEW YORK TIMES*, 1998

A NEW MAGAZINE FOR A NEW AGE
DAVID FRIEND

28

Fig.28
Vanity Fair cover, inaugural issue,
by Milton Glaser, March 1983

The first three covers of the
relaunched magazine used
illustrations, echoing the spirit
of its Jazz Age predecessor.

Vanity Fair lay dormant for nearly half a century. But the magazine seemed ready to be roused from slumber. A vibrant cosmopolitan spirit was coursing through the culture in the early 1980s. And, believing that a revamped and resurrected *Vanity Fair* might perfectly suit the times, S.I. Newhouse, Jr, chairman of the Condé Nast Publications, sought to bring it back to life. He had a hunch that the title's prestigious legacy in the arts – including its knack for creating photographic icons of the high and mighty – would still hold sway in sophisticated circles.

The go-go 1980s and 1990s would soon become something of a mirror of the Jazz Age, the hothouse era that had given the earlier *Vanity Fair* its sizzle – and its talent pool of writers, illustrators and photographers. In 1983, as the magazine was relaunched, Silicon Valley and Wall Street were buoyant, high society was in full swing, and men and women of maverick vision and social standing were making their mark. (By 1987, their ranks would be savagely lampooned in Tom Wolfe's aptly titled novel *The Bonfire of the Vanities*.) In addition, the art market was exploding. Advertising was ascendant. Everyone from

politicians to restaurateurs employed image consultants. And nightlife was thriving, riding the coattails of the decadent 1970s, though the AIDS pandemic had just begun to cast its pall.

Newhouse's notion seemed a safe enough bet. Celebrity culture had secured such a hold on the contemporary psyche that the art of 'presenting personalities', according to Condé Nast editorial director Alexander Liberman, had become 'the obsession of our time'. Photographic portraiture increasingly occupied museum and gallery walls and fuelled the fashion world, where runway waifs had morphed into supermodels. Movie and TV stars dominated the pages of magazines like *People*, which had been introduced the decade before. As new, industry-shifting platforms arose for entertainment and information – the Walkman and Game Boy, the CD and camcorder, satellite television and Blockbuster, the Macintosh and MTV – it seemed as if media, in the words of culture critic Frank Rich, had usurped nature as 'America's backdrop'. Media consumers, in turn, became more and more preoccupied with the personal narratives of the figures that permeated this ever-present overlay of video clips,

audio streams, and computer and movie screens.

In this environment, there appeared to be an audience eager for a tasteful, high-end, general-interest glossy, for a publication that could elevate actors (De Niro, Streep) into the same lofty orbit as artists (Lichtenstein, Salle) and authors (García Márquez, Milosz), as *Vanity Fair* did in its inaugural issue in March 1983 (fig.28). Café society might have gone the way of the speakeasy, but there was now a burgeoning cachet society, an elite group of personalities in diverse areas of endeavour that was connecting with a diverse readership, one that felt somehow privileged because of that connection. The celebrated were our picture-perfect surrogates, our magnified, wealthier, airbrushed selves.

In a manner of speaking, the stars had aligned. In 1981, Ronald Reagan, the former film actor and governor of California, stormed into the White House, giving the capital a dose of Hollywood glamour. Reagan's reliance on image over depth mirrored the culture's. His spin team mastered the photo op. His policies were parcelled out in sound bites. His slogans ('evil empire', 'Go ahead, make my day') were lifted directly from the movies. He knew that the electorate preferred surface to substance – the latter demanding too much concentration and nuance in a world wired for easy dichotomies: West vs. East, Good vs. Evil, Yes vs. Just Say No.

There was no better time to launch a publication of highbrow sensibility, irreverent tone, brisk pacing and photographic splash, which covered the culture's monthly panoply, chronicled the vertiginous thrills and risks of success, and explored the fascinating disconnects between public image and private life. The magazine, wrote *Newsweek*, 'had the chance to define fin de siècle America the way Frank Crowninshield's *Vanity Fair* captured the 20s'.

Despite this promising setting, however, the revived *Vanity Fair* had a difficult birth. Its first two editors, Richard Locke and Leo Lerman, produced an unlucky thirteen issues between them. Their magazine was too high-minded for the times, lacking a clear editorial vision, true wit, and a solid graphic and photographic grounding. The editors called upon established masters of the glamour shot (Hiro, Horst P. Horst, George Hurrell and Bert Stern) and photographers renowned not only for their editorial work but also for fine art triumphs (Richard Avedon, David

Hockney [fig.29], Andy Warhol and Irving Penn).

Yet the editors' chosen subjects were sometimes out of phase with the Zeitgeist. Four straight covers, for example, displayed strong Penn headshots of intellectuals: looming close-ups, cocooned in black and silver shadow, projecting the cold monumentality of Roman busts. Neither readers nor advertisers seemed keen to have Philip Roth's stubble (fig.30) or Italo Calvino's nose hair grace their coffee tables for a month.

New Republic critic Henry Fairlie was scathing in his review of *Vanity Fair*'s initial effort: 'There are *People*-length tributes to Elizabeth Hardwick, to John Huston, to V.S. Pritchett, all very deserving people, but why *them*, now, in March 1983? … They are thrown in as little dollops of culture, olives in the martini, for what culture is to the new *Vanity Fair*, which it never was to the old, is busy name dropping.'

Editors' Fresh Eyes

The idea behind *Vanity Fair* seemed ripe, nonetheless. So a determined Mr Newhouse conscripted Christina Hambley Brown – Tina, she was called – a saucy, savvy editor from England (by way of *Punch*, *The Times* and

Tatler), to take charge. Brown understood how to calibrate rapid-fire word and image so as to echo the pulse of the modern age. She abhorred the notion, as she put it, 'that visual excitement is somehow at odds with intellectual content', and would eventually assert that '*V.F.* is the quintessential postmodern magazine. It is the great high-low show: Demi Moore's pregnant belly side by side with Martha Graham's dance aesthetic.'

Brown set about mixing her magazine's ingredients: celebrity profiles, high-society scandal, all manner of decadence, high-calibre reportage, literary firepower. She courted authority figures and power players. She valued the elegant and refined, yet strove for controversy. And, as did the earlier *V.F.*, Brown's depended on inventive photography – the graphic bedrock of the magazine. High-impact portraits of personalities would appeal to the modern-day reader accustomed to overstimulation and instant gratification in the warp-speed, ad-addled, visual age.

Vanity Fair assigned the acclaimed Robert Mapplethorpe, nightlife mainstays Dafydd Jones and Roxanne Lowit, established Hollywood talent Herb Ritts, the photojournalistically inclined such

as Jonathan Becker, Harry Benson, Elliott Erwitt and Mary Ellen Mark, chroniclers of eros and edge such as Michel Comte, Bill King and Helmut Newton. What's more, the new magazine settled on one photographer to be its chief image-maker. Annie Leibovitz was wooed away from *Rolling Stone*, even before Brown arrived, with the promise that she would be *V.F.*'s latter-day Edward Steichen, just as the 'modern' Steichen had been wooed into the Condé Nast fold in 1923 (to replace the dusty Baron De Meyer when his soft-focused style was on the wane). Her provocative photographs – along with the bold prose of writers such as T.D. Allman, Marie Brenner, Bob Colacello, Dominick Dunne, Maureen Orth, Gail Sheehy and James Wolcott – would come to epitomize the 1980s magazine.

Even so, Brown struggled. Despite her editorial daring and infusion of talented contributors, she failed to attract a requisite influx of readers. Proprietor Newhouse, reportedly, was beginning to lose patience and was said to have told intimates in 1985 that *Vanity Fair* was in danger of being shelved, possibly for good. And then, at the eleventh hour, the magazine managed to land two transformative photo sessions.

Fig.31
'I'm The Guy They Called
Deep Throat', photograph
by Gasper Tringale
Vanity Fair, July 2005

In a world exclusive, the magazine revealed
that Mark Felt, an ex-FBI official, was 'Deep
Throat', the confidential source of the 1970s
Watergate scandal that forced President
Richard Nixon from office.

Fig.29
Self-portrait, *Vanity Fair* cover
by David Hockney, June 1983

Fig.30
Philip Roth, *Vanity Fair* cover
by Irving Penn, September 1983

Benson's Breakthrough

First, *Vanity Fair*'s editors had persuaded President and Mrs Reagan to carve a smidgen out of their schedules to accommodate a camera as the First Couple, in formal attire, made their entrance to a White House state dinner. Yet unbeknownst to the president's press liaisons, who were off retrieving the Reagans, *V.F.* photographer Harry Benson had gone a step further, craftily setting up a white backdrop. 'Their aides would have turned me down', he recalls, 'had I mentioned the concept beforehand – but once the thing was set in motion, they were afraid to interrupt.' The intensely focused Benson, who had taken portraits of every president since Eisenhower, held his breath and his Minolta and awaited his prey.

Reagan, in a tux, and the First Lady, wearing a black sequinned gown, approached. Benson saw them from afar and gave a signal. An assistant flipped on a tape player. In an intoxicating wave, Frank Sinatra's 'Nancy (With the Laughing Face)' wafted across the room and Benson ushered them into position.

By serenading Nancy Reagan with a favourite song performed by her favourite singer, Benson was able to coax six minutes from the pair as they danced and twirled and even kissed for the camera. At one point the First Lady, in the jaunty mood of the moment, flicked her high heel like a 1920s flapper. Benson's rendering of that instant – the elegant Reagans embracing, a vision of how Hollywood might have portrayed the ultimate Washington power couple (p.155) – sashayed onto *V.F.*'s June 1985 cover.

'The Reagan cover', wrote journalist Thomas Maier, 'was a big hit and was eventually recalled as one of the crucial moments when *Vanity Fair* turned away from the financial abyss. "[They] put us on the map," Brown said later of the presidential coup. "They gave Mr Newhouse cause to think there was light at the end of the tunnel." The Reagans, true to the decade whose style they personified, had helped to save the magazine that would chronicle all of its excess and splendor.'

Next, right on the Reagans' heels, so to speak, came Helmut Newton's shocking photographs, published that same summer, of socialite Claus von Bülow, first bedecked in black leather (p.141), next posing with his new companion, Andrea Reynolds, then doing a crude imitation of Queen Victoria, even though he was on trial for the second time for attempting to murder his wife, Sunny, who lay in a coma. (Von Bülow was acquitted.) *Vanity Fair*, through the high-wattage jolt of its photos, had hit a cultural trip wire. Buzz for the magazine began to build. The press and the advertising community came clamouring. And Newhouse, his initial inkling validated, decided to keep the picture show going.

Some of the magazine's best-remembered images of the 1980s and early 1990s tended to be suggestive and sexually charged. Steven Meisel depicted actress Daryl Hannah as a Barbarella-esque temptress in a futuristic wet suit (p.162). Photographer Bill King's Raquel Welch was enveloped in a damp, campy scrum of naked male Olympians (p.142). Though *Vanity Fair* sometimes kowtowed to the Reagans and their coterie, Brown gleefully ran a Leibovitz shot of First Son Ron cavorting in his underwear. This was followed by Benson photos of First Daughter Patti Davis in bed with a teddy bear, spilling out of a sheer, low-cut dress. (The introduction to the Davis story seemed to put a perverse love-hate spin on some 1960s sitcom: 'The most estranged member of America's favorite dysfunctional family ...'.)

The Washington Post

Nixon Resigns
Ford Assumes Presidency Today

GRANDPA G-MAN
Former F.B.I. official
W. Mark Felt, 91, is now a
retiree living in Santa Rosa,
California. He has told friends
and intimates that he was the
confidential inside source
of Watergate fame.

"I'M THE GUY THEY CALLED DEEP THROAT"

Despite three decades of intense speculation, the identity of "Deep Throat"—
the source who leaked key details of Nixon's Watergate cover-up to *Washington Post*
reporters Bob Woodward and Carl Bernstein—has never been revealed.
Now, at age 91, W. Mark Felt, number two at the F.B.I. in the early 70s, is finally
admitting to that historic, anonymous role. In an exclusive,
JOHN D. O'CONNOR puts a name and face to one of American democracy's heroes,
learning about the struggle between honor and duty that nearly led Felt
to take his secret to the grave

O n a sunny California morning in August 1999, Joan Felt, a busy college Spanish professor and single mother, was completing chores before leaving for class. She stopped when she heard an unexpected knock at the front door. Upon answering it, she was met by a courteous, 50-ish man, who introduced himself as a journalist from *The Washington Post.* He asked if he could see her father, W. Mark Felt, who lived with her in her suburban Santa Rosa home. The man said his name was Bob Woodward.
Woodward's name did not register with Joan, and she assumed he was no different from a number of other reporters, who had called that week. This was, after all, the 25th anniversary of the resignation of President Richard Nixon, disgraced in the scandal known as Watergate, and hounded from office in 1974. The journalists had all

PHOTOGRAPH BY GASPER TRINGALE

The magazine's subjects, in concert with *V.F.*'s photographers, were pushing photo sessions to their limits in a performance-art satire of their own celebrity. The images – Lauren Hutton wrestling an alligator (by Newton); Princess Caroline of Monaco, in tiara and royal-blue gown, clutching a diaper-clad baby (by Karl Lagerfeld, p.159) – were a wink to the reader: postmodern fame was sometimes sustained or amplified by letting the viewer lift the curtain on the artifice required to maintain one's public persona.

Through portraits on a page, stargazers possessed the stars as keepsakes. '[Our] culture invests so much of its energy creating, consuming and obsessing about photographic images', observed curators Carole Kismaric and Marvin Heiferman, that 'today, fame can't exist without photography.' The lives and stories of the earthbound gravitated toward the lives and stories of their idols, like tiny moons around heavenly bodies.

Soon, Maier would note, *Vanity Fair*, responding to this fascination, 'became one of the most influential publications of its era, covering it all with a high-gloss eroticism and slightly decadent insiderish voice, like some giant traveling circus from prewar Berlin. The singular

impact of *Vanity Fair* – and its unique view of just how the 1980s looked and felt to the nation – was immeasurable, with media from august newspapers to TV's "Lifestyles of the Rich and Famous" seeming to emulate its style.'

Bold Growth

The periodical, however, was not yet a financial powerhouse (even though an overseas *Vanity Fair* had been launched out of London in 1990). At the same time, Condé Nast's *New Yorker* was off its editorial game. And so Newhouse, in 1992, despatched Brown to rejuvenate that magazine and enlisted Graydon Carter – a veteran of both *Time* and *Life*, co-founder of the inimitable *Spy*, and editor of *The New York Observer* – to try his hand at *V.F.*'s helm. He had a shrewd news sense and cultural intuition, but he struggled for a year or so before synchronizing his own editorial voice and tastes with the magazine's. Soon, Carter, with his charm, Falstaffian sociability and ravenous curiosity (the latter trait possessed, not surprisingly, by all great photographers), brought the magazine to new levels of journalistic prowess, photographic ambition and profitability.

He expanded the magazine's coverage of news and world affairs, especially in the aftermath of the 9/11 attacks. He added contributors of intellectual heft: Robert Sam Anson, Buzz Bissinger, Bryan Burrough, Amy Fine Collins (who began to write long-form pieces), David Halberstam, Christopher Hitchens, Sebastian Junger, William Langewiesche, David Margolick, Todd Purdum and Michael Wolff among them. He inaugurated new franchises that have become *V.F.* cornerstones: extensive business coverage (creating the New Establishment rankings), fashion expertise (as the guardians of the International Best-Dressed List) and the perennial Hollywood Issue (along with the magazine's star-studded Oscar gala, which has evolved into the most celebrated annual party in the world). With *V.F.*'s dinner and after-party on Academy Awards night, Carter became the master of the perfectly hosted 21st-century social event: an unparalleled gathering of modern men and women of culture, stature and talent from myriad fields and cities – a living enactment of the personalities photographed for the pages of the magazine.

Wittingly or not, Carter was acting upon his forebear Frank

Crowninshield's dictum, laid out in a 1914 editor's letter: 'Take a dozen or so cultivated men and women; dress them becomingly; sit them down to dinner.... What will these people say? … *Vanity Fair* is that dinner!'

In time, Carter's magazine became the publishing world's acknowledged arbiter of power, personality and society, and a monthly must-see among tastemakers and trendsetters in the corridors of influence around the globe. *Vanity Fair*, observed David Carr of *The New York Times*, 'sits atop the American magazine industry. Beneath *Vanity Fair*'s louche exterior lies the beating heart of a well-financed, well-edited enterprise that has managed to break news as a monthly at a time when the news cycle is frequently measured in minutes. In [2005–6], the magazine has revealed the identity of Deep Throat [fig.31], had an exclusive interview with the disgraced lobbyist Jack Abramoff and disclosed big celebrity news despite the fierce competition of swarming weeklies.'

Vanity Fair also became an ever more bounteous eyeful. Marquee-name portraitists came on board to join Leibovitz and Co. – Patrick Demarchelier, Jonas Karlsson, David LaChapelle, Mark Seliger,

A handful of the boys who have walked thousands of miles through southern Sudan in search of sanctuary.

THE LAST PLACE ON EARTH

In the ravaged beauty of southern Sudan, writer
ROGER ROSENBLATT and photographer SEBASTIÃO SALGADO
found a world ending without even a whisper

Snowdon, Mario Testino, Bruce Weber, along with fashion and style director Michael Roberts – giving *V.F.* the most formidable photographic roster in the business. The lavish picture spreads they produced felt even more enticing and seductive than the adjacent advertisements.

The magazine's photographic palette expanded to include reportage (Sebastião Salgado in war-torn Rwanda and Sudan [fig.32]; James Nachtwey in Vietnam and Indonesia) and architectural photography (often by Todd Eberle). Its multi-page portfolios (of explorers, sports figures, power brokers and the like) were widely mimicked. Award nominations were bestowed on the publication for special sections heralding heroes in times of tragedy (the volunteers at Ground Zero after 9/11; the humanitarian effort in the wake of Hurricane Katrina).

At times, the leading figures of the day were registered in the social retina by how they were rendered through *V.F.*'s lens. *Vanity Fair* photo sessions would help shape the way the world viewed everyone from Jack Nicholson (p.186), to Helen Mirren (p.156), to Rupert Murdoch (p.208). Madonna, the Merlin of public image, would appear on *V.F.*'s

cover a record nine times, in part to test-run her roles as ingénue, sex-book purveyor, serious actress, new mother (fig.33).

In situations for which a news weekly or a TV news magazine might have been granted exclusive access in years past, it was now *Vanity Fair* that would be invited inside: for the first portrait of President Bill Clinton in office (in 1993); for the formal group shot of President George W. Bush's Afghan-war Cabinet (in 2001, p.209); for an at-home visit with the fiercely private Vice President Dick Cheney as the Iraq war raged (in 2006). When *V.F.*, in 1998, secured a much-coveted photo session with Monica Lewinsky, the intern at the heart of the Clinton White House sex scandal, *New York Times* columnist Maureen Dowd declared, 'Getting your own photo shoot in Vanity Fair has become the premier achievement in our celebrity-mad culture.' (The three best-selling covers in *V.F.*'s history featured Jennifer Aniston [fig.34], Tom Cruise and his family [p.223] and Carolyn Bessette Kennedy [fig.35].) Carter would concur: 'The pages of *Vanity Fair*, more than any other two-dimensional space in our culture, have taken on a status equivalent to the High Sierra of the Public Image…. Many of the

magazine's most memorable photographs are, in fact, the iconic images of their subjects.'

The Skin Game

Then, of course, there is the *Vanity Fair* cover as provocation. For Carter's second cover story, in November 1992 ('Liz Aid: Elizabeth Taylor's AIDS Odyssey', shot by Firooz Zahedi), the actress promoted 'safe sex' by brandishing a condom. The following summer Herb Ritts would shoot model Cindy Crawford playing a barber, blissfully cradling to her breast the beaming face of musician k.d. lang, in drag (fig.36). Over the years, *V.F.* façades have featured men's abs (Heath Ledger, David Beckham, Brad Pitt), double-take-inducing cover lines ('Does Cleavage Sell Magazines?' – cosily abutting a come-hither Jennifer Aniston) and ample nudity. Leibovitz's March 2006 Hollywood Issue cover (outtake, p.228) juxtaposed two of cinema's hottest young stars, Scarlett Johansson and Keira Knightley, in the altogether, the latter being nuzzled by fashion mogul Tom Ford, fully clothed, in a send-up of Edouard Manet's radical painting *Déjeuner sur l'Herbe*, which had caused an uproar

Fig.32
'The Last Place on Earth', photograph
by Sebastião Salgado
Vanity Fair, July 1993

Over the years the publication has
expanded its coverage of conflict and
world affairs.

– in 1863 – for its frank exploration of sexual politics.

There was a seduction implied in the artifice, in the dressing up and the undressing, in the slick pages themselves. A photograph that shows a star staring into the lens gives off the air of flirtation. And over the last generation, many images have involved less clothes and more skin. All participants in Hollywood's Eros eco-system understand the formula: when it comes to pictures, sex connects and generates maximum buzz more quickly than any other visual trapping, attitude or contrivance.

In all, twenty-six men and women have posed topless or undressed for the cover. The female breast, with irrepressible regularity, has been cupped or caressed or allowed to peep through flimsy cloth. A pigtailed, 1950s-style Madonna, by Steven Meisel, appeared on one cover as a barely legal tease in a kiddie's pink inner tube (fig.33d); Herb Ritts had model Cindy Crawford assume the role of a naked Venus on the half shell. Annie Leibovitz depicted a muscle-bound Sylvester Stallone as Rodin's *Thinker* (in a pose reminiscent of *V.F.* photographer Ira L. Hill's 1923 image of boxer Jack Dempsey) and, for the magazine's very first Hollywood Issue, in 1995, she

asked the likes of Uma Thurman, Nicole Kidman and Sarah Jessica Parker to wear an array of clinging gowns and lingerie.

Cover Story

Probably the most controversial cover in modern magazine history was the one on *Vanity Fair*'s August 1991 issue: Leibovitz's study of a disrobed Demi Moore, seven-months pregnant with her daughter Scout, shielding her breasts and proudly displaying her belly (p.165). The cover, subliminally referencing antecedents from Botticelli to Benetton, showed Moore as the embodiment of empowered female sexuality – Earth Mother as Hot Madonna. And it caused a firestorm. Some stores embargoed it. Issues in some states were sheathed in paper wrappers to avoid offending news-stand patrons. News broadcasts followed the hue and cry.

'I thought about how people in this country don't want to embrace motherhood and sensuality', Moore would explain. 'While you're pregnant you're made to feel not beautiful or sexually viable. You're either sexy or you're a mother. I didn't want to have to choose, so I challenged that.' In terms of cross-cultural recognition

and infamy, that cover, along with a second nude appearance twelve months later (in which a slimmed-down Moore posed in body paint), 'had the impact of two hit movies', wrote *Interview* magazine.

'So much of the work is about sex', says Susan White, *Vanity Fair*'s photography director and a two-decade veteran of the magazine. 'Herb, Helmut, Bruce Weber. Many photographers admit they get into photography as a way to meet girls – or boys. Many of them do. But then they go on to reveal themselves, their psyches, through the landscape of their work.'

Sex, naturally, is humanity's oldest sales tool. And in the magazine business the cover is as much about ensuring a given issue's newsstand appeal as it is about artful imagery or savvy packaging or an editor defining a brand. To that end, film personalities portrayed in an alluring, magnetic way have been the magazine's subjects of choice since the mid-1980s. As the critic and *V.F.* contributor James Wolcott posits, 'Movie stars dominate the covers of *Vanity Fair* not only because their good looks are enticing but also because Hollywood [has become] the international Valhalla of vanity, the pagan temple and world capital of mass illusion and myth.

Hollywood's faces are the most recognizable form of currency in our entertainment culture.'

'The cover of *Time*', he notes, 'reigned for decades as the most telling and enshrining social indicator, but now that the news magazines peddle so many service-oriented bulletins – Shoes: Everyone's Wearing Them! – *Vanity Fair* monopolizes the mirror of our media existence. Covers seduce [the readers into its pages, while] the sonar depth of the magazine's writing and reporting … keeps the faces of the pretty and powerful afloat in the pool of Narcissus.'

American Photo magazine, placing it all in context, asserted that *Vanity Fair* 'is arguably the grandest showcase of photography in the world. [Graydon] Carter has devoted pages to serious photojournalism and seriously covered photography as an art [and] has charted a unique course in publishing that has made the magazine our most important journal, not only of pop culture but also photography.'

Leibovitz: Her Imprint and Impact

No single photographer in the late twentieth century has had a greater influence on portraiture

Fig.33 a–i.

Vanity Fair covers of Madonna:

a) by Herb Ritts, December 1986
b) by Helmut Newton, April 1990
c) by Steven Meisel, April 1991
d) by Steven Meisel, October 1992
e) by Mario Testino, November 1996
f) by Mario Testino, March 1998
g) by Mario Testino, March 2000
(Madonna with Rupert Everett)
h) by Craig McDean, October 2002
i) by Annie Leibovitz, July 2007
(Madonna with Djimon Hounsou)

Madonna has appeared on Vanity Fair's cover a record nine times – ten, if one counts her appearance on two alternate Africa Issue covers.

than Annie Leibovitz. Her pictures, first for Rolling Stone and since 1983 for Vanity Fair and Vogue – along with her advertising campaigns for companies such as American Express – have made her the most imitated image-maker of her generation, and the most famous. (A wax Leibovitz, focusing a Mamiya camera, is enshrined in Manhattan's Madame Tussauds.) Remarkably, Annie Leibovitz, who has put her imprint on nearly 130 Vanity Fair covers, consistently turns a personality's image into a fixture in our collective visual unconscious. 'What other contemporary photographer', Newsweek asked recently, 'has produced as many indelible images of American pop culture?'

Leibovitz has helped bring about several trends in modern portraiture. First, she excels at concentrating on one or more distinguishing features of a famous subject (a prop, a trademark gesture, an affectation) and then uses those elements, sometimes taken to the extreme, to render that person iconographically. In many of her best photographs, her subjects assume their public image in much the same way that an actor assumes a character's essence in the mind of a film- or theatregoer.

To distill the persona of Whoopi Goldberg, for example, Leibovitz persuaded the then budding comedian-monologist-actress to slide into a bathtub brimming with milk. As Goldberg's mischievous grin and limbs peep out of the tub, she becomes the Comic Emergent, an African-American woman surfacing from the depths of the white-dominated comedy world (fig.37). 'When that picture came out [in 1984],' Goldberg has said, 'everything changed, literally overnight, where I was walking down the street on Friday night, just walking down the street. And Saturday morning people were yelling my name.'

'The photographer's great fear is that the patient will say, "No"', insists John Loengard, Life's former picture editor. 'Steichen was fearless in a formal studio setting, asking Norma Shearer to put on a particular gown or Charlie Chaplin to take aim with his cane, pretending to shoot at his hat. Annie, by working with her Rolling Stone background, hanging out with rock 'n' rollers, developed a "no fear" attitude toward performers and celebrities – and a confidence in feeling that what she wanted would work well. There are no rules in rock 'n' roll. There were few publicists around. Rock stars

became bigger before your eyes, like mushrooms growing overnight, their fame coming on so fast.'

In the early 1980s, Loengard believes, Leibovitz brought that bravado to her Vanity Fair sessions, an impulse to push the conceptual envelope that had been largely foreign to portrait-taking and had more connection with other genres: performance art, experimental film, edgy television commercials and over-the-top fashion photography. 'This was a new level of purity of imagination in portraiture', he asserts. 'It popped out of nowhere. And she's been expanding her range ever since, working around an idea, a concept, refining it, until she gets what she wants.' (Indeed, Leibovitz acknowledges that a 1981 Life assignment commissioned by Loengard – a portfolio of American poets for which she shot Robert Penn Warren with his shirt off and Tess Gallagher in a spangled gown, on horseback – was a turning point in her development as a portraitist testing the limits of her subjects and the medium.)

It Takes Two

A second distinguishing talent is Leibovitz's willingness to engage her sitters in a collaborative effort.

Often, they are part of the creative process, giving her photographs added intimacy and energy. Her subjects feel more inclined to let their guard down – publicists and handlers notwithstanding – if they've been welcomed into what is typically a one-sided transaction, in which the person behind the camera wields most of the power. That collaboration, however, goes only so far. Leibovitz typically harbours a hidden concept – perhaps an homage to another photograph, painting or cultural reference – that adds a subtext to the image and, on occasion, an astute level of criticism.

During a 1986 Leibovitz session, avant-garde director David Lynch stood beside actress-muse Isabella Rossellini and pulled a black turtleneck over his face, allowing the photographer to create a Surrealist scene redolent of a René Magritte canvas. In 1994, tennis player Martina Navratilova assumed the role of the Human Form Triumphant, her body taut as she tugged a giant circular gear – in a re-creation of Lewis Hine's classic 1920 image of a steamfitter, one of a series that recorded life in the steel-making district of Pittsburgh and a celebration of Human Labour (figs 38, 39).

A Leibovitz cover is often an homage to an iconic photograph, from her take of Will Smith on a rearing horse in 1999 (referencing Life's 1943 Walter Sanders cover of Roy Rogers and Trigger) to her October 2006 portrait of Tom Cruise cradling his newborn baby, Suri, in the folds of his coat (echoing Linda McCartney's shot of husband Paul, with Stella), to Julia Roberts as a forest nymph (reminiscent of Penn's 1948 study Ballet Society, New York).

In 1997, for one of her most graphically rewarding covers, Leibovitz shot Arnold Schwarzenegger, another actor who later served as California's governor (p.187). Ski poles in hand, he stands on a snowcapped slope. His sculpted muscles ripple under a white T-shirt as his gaze, hidden by sunglasses, seems to point slightly skyward. Schwarzenegger is affecting the classic posture of the mountaineer-athlete, a specimen of human perfection poised gallantly at the top of the world. But whether the Austrian-born actor knew it or not, he was also visually signifying the 1930s Aryan ideal: Leibovitz's image was clearly inspired by the portraiture of the German actress-outdoorswoman turned filmmaker, Leni Riefenstahl, who would become the Third Reich's chief iconographer (p.81).

In recent years, Leibovitz, who professes a debt to Henri Cartier-Bresson and Robert Frank, has made decidedly documentary images – stripped down, spontaneous, raw. She can come in on a subject in his or her environment, with little flourish: Bill Gates at his computer, Bruce Springsteen composing. Like the best documentarians, she focuses not only on the centre but also the periphery, anticipating the revelatory gesture or expression or an exquisite compositional tension. And yet, she is careful to point out, she doesn't consider herself a photojournalist. 'A journalist doesn't take sides', she has written, 'and I don't want to go through life like that. I have a more powerful voice as a photographer if I express a point of view.'

At the other extreme, many of her best pictures attain a painterly cast and complexity. Her subjects are often depicted in full figure, their bodies frequently set against ornate backgrounds. Many of her recent portraits, for all their inner fluidity, are painstakingly composed mini-dramas enacted for the camera. Most are flawlessly illuminated in the manner of neoclassical masters such as Gainsborough or Ingres, her subjects, such as Nicole Kidman (p.192), appearing eerily radiant at times, almost translucent, as if shimmering from some cool inner light source. Her image of a reclining Sofia Coppola (p.212) has a dreamlike cast, the product of luscious shadow, suffused colour, and an intimacy and tenderness that are almost palpable.

What's more, her subjects' moods are pensive, resolute, occasionally ethereal or aloof or sombre. Only rarely does a smile appear on one of her Vanity Fair covers after 1993. Leibovitz seems to have made a conscious effort, starting in the early 1990s, to create portraits of more profound consequence, images that draw on the full range of emotions surging in the souls of her subjects – and herself. The worlds within her images have become more serious and multi-layered (she documented conflicts in war-torn Bosnia and Rwanda for the magazine in 1994), reflecting her own maturation as an artist and the tension and gravity of the world outside the frame.

'She's an aesthete', contends V.F. design director David Harris, 'the chiaroscuro, the formalism. There's a grace in her photographs that no one else can capture. She cares about the aesthetics, and yet there's great humanity. And she has a quest for perfection. I've never known anyone to be

Fig.34
Jennifer Aniston, *Vanity Fair* cover
by Mario Testino, September 2005

Fig.35
Carolyn Bessette Kennedy,
Vanity Fair cover by Bruce Weber,
September 1999

The three best-selling covers in
the history of *Vanity Fair* featured
Jennifer Aniston, Tom Cruise and
family (p.223, image from cover
story) and Carolyn Bessette Kennedy.

more emblematic of the truth
that if she wasn't doing her art,
she wouldn't exist.'

Lofty Constellations

Through it all, Annie Leibovitz has
used *Vanity Fair* as a medium
for conveying the pageantry and
folly of titanic personalities. And
in this regard, there is no better
photographic canvas than the
group portrait. Her elaborate
gatherings – most notably her
multi-panel gatefolds that have
graced the annual *V.F.* Hollywood
Issue since 1995 – have become
a signature of the magazine. With
such covers, along with select
spreads and foldouts (for example,
her virtuoso 33-page movie-in-a-
magazine, photographed in 2007,
as a sequence of would-be *noir*
film stills; as well as her study of the
cast of HBO's *The Sopranos*
re-enacting Leonardo da Vinci's
The Last Supper), the monopoly
over the epic group shot has
passed from *Life* and *Esquire*
of the 1950s and 1960s to the
modern-day *Vanity Fair*.
    Leibovitz's 2001 Hollywood Issue
double gatefold (p.198) was one
of her most ambitious cover shoots,
not only because of the logistical
challenges of photographing ten
A-list actresses – Cate Blanchett,

Penélope Cruz, Nicole Kidman,
Catherine Deneuve, Sophia Loren,
Gwyneth Paltrow, Meryl Streep
Vanessa Redgrave, Kate Winslet
and Chloë Sevigny – in three
locations, no less (New York,
Los Angeles and London). Most
impressive of all was the way she
conceived and executed the
triptych as a single orchestrated
image. 'Knowing that the three
component photos … would be
stitched together digitally,' wrote
American Photo, 'Leibovitz took
special care to position her …
softboxes so that the lighting was
absolutely constant from session to
session. Note the light's seamless
"falloff" from the left side of the
image to the right. This is what
makes the photo look as if it was
shot all at once in a supernova
of celebrity.'
    Decreed *The New York Times*,
apropos of images by Leibovitz,
Mark Seliger, Art Streiber,
Norman Jean Roy and others:
'The Vanity Fair group portrait is
today's equivalent of Parnassus,
where glorified talents come to
pose.' They are arrangements,
says James Wolcott, 'of famous
musicians, actors … athletes …
and politicians, as if they were
members of an 18th-century
salon, an aristocracy of talent
whose achievements intertwine.'
Such juxtapositions took on an

added resonance in a 2007
special issue on Africa, for which
Leibovitz shot twenty separate
covers over six weeks on three
continents, pairing the likes of
Archbishop Desmond Tutu and
actor Brad Pitt, US Secretary of
State Condoleezza Rice and Bono.
    'I was at the 2007 Hollywood
cover shoot', says features editor
Jane Sarkin, who has set up more
than 500 sessions with Leibovitz –
and arranged every *Vanity Fair*
cover over the last two decades.
'Out of nowhere she said to me, as
she was about to shoot, "Watch
the magic begin". She'd never said
anything like that before.
    'What she meant was that
she thinks about a shoot so long
before she does it – the research
of looking at historical pictures, the
preparation, everything to the nth
degree – that once she actually
gets behind that camera, it all
comes together: the magazine,
the power of the people she's
photographing, and her eye.
    'The [electric] fans start going,
the music in the studio is turned
up, the only voice you hear is
hers', Sarkin continues. 'The hair
is in her face as she's thinking,
leaning over, pacing. She walks
over to you and arranges your
lapel. She moves here and there.
That energy of creation – that's the
magic that becomes a picture.'

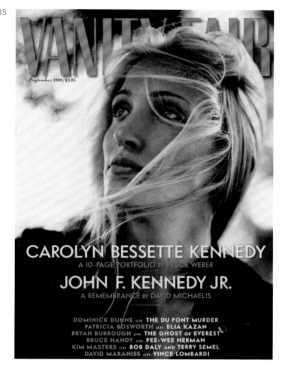

Vanity Fair Auteurs

In the Jazz Age *Vanity Fair*, photographers tended to render their subjects formally, in a studio environment, usually divorced from the real world. Their images were ideas. Their subjects were objects, frozen in space and light and shadow, sometimes depicted in reverie – the better to accommodate the pokey shutter speed.

Vanity Fair pictures were often patterned like paintings. Some of the magazine's early photographers had been trained as artists. Baron De Meyer, like various contemporaries, was known to sign his portraits. Man Ray, a pioneer of Dada – and the magazine's Paris shooter – straddled the divide between the worlds of art and editorial photography (though he would later complain that 'the debatable art of [portrait] photography [forced him to be] invaded by all kinds of people who came to see me as though I were a doctor'). Edward Steichen was an established curator and artist and, along with De Meyer, George Hoyningen-Huene and others, earned a sizable portion of his income shooting fashion and advertising. Cecil Beaton did illustrations, costume design, stage

and movie sets and scenery.

Shooting during the 1910s and 1920s – when modern art, music and dance were germinating – these portraitists generally produced images that were as much about form, and about experimenting with format, as they were about substance. Style often subsumed subject. Come the mid-to-late-1920s, many of these 'modernist' images were spare and clean, marked by chiselled lines, bold shadows and geometric stridency.

In contrast, by the time of the current-era *V.F.*, most of the conventions of so-called celebrity portraiture had been firmly established. Mass-produced images of royals, statesmen and show-business figures – in the form of trading-card-style *cartes de visite* – had begun circulating as early as the 1860s. The 1920s and 1930s saw a tabloid boom and the invention of portable 35mm cameras, which spurred the birth of photojournalism. (Indeed, *Life* was launched in 1936, the same year that *Vanity Fair* suspended publication.)

Come the 1940s and 1950s, environmental portraiture, pioneered by photographers such as Arnold Newman, came into its own, as famous subjects shared the frame with the accoutrements of

their private, creative or workaday surroundings, and photographers attempted to use atmosphere, telling details and spatial relationships to reveal deeper truths about a sitter's life, work and values. After the emergence in the 1950s of television, television advertising and colour photography in the hands of the masses, there followed in the 1960s the rise of the counter-culture and free love, and in the 1970s and 1980s rampant celebrity worship. The stage was set at the turn of the millennium for an approach to photographic portraiture that was influenced by the immediacy of candid photography and the Internet, the slickness of television and film, the exhibitionism and hedonism of the rock and fashion worlds and the quick-sell, icon-in-an-instant imperatives of Madison Avenue.

The subjects of *Vanity Fair* pictures from the 1980s to the present day are often the photographers' co-conspirators. Unlike their 1920s and 1930s predecessors, they are not prone to affect sidelong glances so as to maintain the pretence of having been caught unawares. Instead, they are apt to peer directly into the lens, acknowledging that they are entirely conscious of being mediated. These personalities

often seem quite comfortable as full partners in the crafting of a believable fiction, which is patterned at times like a fashion layout or an ad campaign or a music video, routinely textured with references to earlier photographs. The end result, understood by all three participants – photographer, sitter and viewer – is that the picture does not relate reality but the artist's best effort at interpreting or amplifying or fashioning the subject's public image.

Art and Commerce

Fashion, indeed. *Vanity Fair* photographers such as Patrick Demarchelier, Annie Leibovitz, Steven Meisel, Helmut Newton, Mario Testino and Bruce Weber have shot some of the best-remembered fashion and advertising spreads of the age – most of them, in fact, running in *Vanity Fair*. Karl Lagerfeld is an influential designer and, like Weber, a book publisher. LaChapelle and Ritts not only created record and CD covers but also directed music videos, commercial spots and, in LaChapelle's case, Las Vegas extravaganzas. (It is interesting to note that photographer Mark

Fig.37
'Making Whoopi', photograph
by Annie Leibovitz
Vanity Fair, July 1984

'When that picture came out,'
comedian Whoopi Goldberg later
remarked, 'everything changed,
literally overnight … on Friday night,
[I was] just walking down the street.
And Saturday morning people were
yelling my name.'

36

Fig.36
Cindy Crawford and k.d. lang,
Vanity Fair cover by Herb Ritts,
August 1993

Seliger, though hardly a fashion-world fixture, has a band and his own photo gallery; Timothy Greenfield-Sanders has a Grammy; Weber, a sometime filmmaker, was a finalist for an Academy Award; Mary Ellen Mark and her husband, Martin Bell, collaborated on the Oscar-nominated documentary *Streetwise*.)

The ad community has borrowed generously from *Vanity Fair*'s pages. To name just one example, a recent Craig McDean shot of model Kate Moss in the buff, reclining in a chair draped in fabric, was re-created using model Mona Johannesson for a Valentino fragrance ad by none other than McDean himself. (Many *V.F.* photographers create the equivalent of a soundstage for their shoots, hauling backdrops, lighting equipment and other gear to far-flung locales, along with legions of assistants and technicians, stylists and make-up artists, prop handlers and catering crews, in what amounts to 'a modern Renaissance court', as designer and director Patrick Kinmonth has described Testino's studio entourage. In so doing, the photographer is able to depict any sitter as if he or she is in a consistently controlled, quasi-cinematic space.)

Fashion shoots, however, don't necessarily prepare a photographer for the demands of portraiture. Fashion models are paid to pose: they exist for the camera, the client, the clothes. Fashion photographers become accustomed to complete authority, to pursuing their every whim.

Celebrity subjects, on the other hand, are often under severe time or editorial constraints, extremely reluctant to participate in certain photographic situations and attended by minders who make their living as rabid guardians of a star's image. And yet, in the hands of an established fashion photographer, a famous sitter can open up, comfortable with the fact that the man or woman behind the camera is practised at catching a subject at his or her most aesthetically and commercially appealing.

'I quite like the idea of commerce and art mixed together', Testino has said. 'However much it is fascinating to have our pictures hanging on walls afterwards and selling as fine art prints, I think that our initial job is to sell clothes and magazines and whatever we're told to sell. For a while I was criticized for it. Some people believe that as photographers we should be more artists than focus on

commerce, but … I prefer seeing my work in a magazine and I like making a difference in how people see something.'

If any fashion-trained portraitist today is considered photographic royalty, it is Testino, who has been said to elicit 'a nonchalant sensual beauty' from his subjects. (When Diana, Princess of Wales, sat for what would be her last major portrait session, twelve weeks before she died in a Paris car crash, the photographer she chose was Testino, his images first published in *Vanity Fair* [p.182]. Her sons, Princes William [p.183] and Harry, later agreed to sit for him as well.)

A Peruvian dynamo, of Italian, Spanish and Irish extraction, he produces images, says *V.F.*'s David Harris, of 'polished, flawless glamour – the most beautiful people you've ever seen in your life – bronzed skin, long legs, fabulous shoes, Mario World. He's got the most voyeuristic vision. He's got that great Latin drive.'

Testino's portraits of Diana and Madonna (p.182; p.218) have 'redefined those most familiar yet elusive faces', writes Kinmonth in Testino's first book, *Any Objections?* Kinmonth argues that even though Testino, as a fashion photographer, 'revels in beautiful surfaces [in a medium] which positively declares its superficiality',

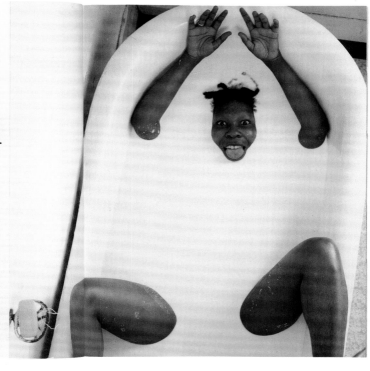

37

The new Lenny Bruce is somewhat different.
She's black.
And she's making a splash.
JANET COLEMAN sees the Whoopi Goldberg variations

Making Whoopi

The bombilation started in New York on February 3, 1984, when the headline WHOOPI GOLDBERG DOES ''THE SPOOK SHOW'' exploded in the ''Weekend'' section of the *Times* above a picture of a grinning black woman and Mel Gussow's rave reviews. Whoopi Goldberg was described as a cross between Lily Tomlin and Richard Pryor, ''not simply a stand-up comedian but a satirist with a cutting edge and an actress with a wry attitude toward life and public performance.''

At the Dance Theater Workshop, in Chelsea, early the following Saturday night, the lines on the staircase included college kids, agents, middle-aged black men in tweed sport coats, old women in minks, and sisters in cornrows. To a dignified experimental theater like D.T.W., *The Spook Show* was obviously more than just a mild sensation. Twenty minutes before curtain, the only seats were on the floor.

For her New York debut, Whoopi Goldberg selected four haunting characters—''spooks''—to appear as a quartet: a dope fiend, a knocked-up surfer chick, a cripple, and a little girl. The dope fiend, Fontaine, opened the show, singing, ''Around the world in ay-tee muh'fuckin' days.'' Scratching his

36

crotch, Fontaine moved into the audience and at once put the crowd at ease and on edge: 'How you doin', mama. That's a bad ring you're wearin'. Want me to hold it for you?''

Back in the spotlight, Fontaine blithely discussed every conceivable controversial subject, from legalized marijuana and Abraham Lincoln to Mr. T (''A guy with a Mohawk I'm supposed to relate to. This motherfucker is a throwback, man'') and aids (''A government conspiracy—they put germs in the discos''). He panned *The Big Chill* as ''a lot of motherfuckers sitting around crying about the sixties. I could have saved them a whole lot of money. Jack. 'Cause I know what happened is the sixties. CETA. You could get a CETA job and learn to part your hair. I see you had one of those jobs.''

Next, this funky Don Quixote ran down a European trip. His spiel was accompanied by a series of eye-popping physical transformations: into a stewardess steering a quivering beverage cart; a microwaved airplane string bean; a German burgher ogling ''the *Schwarze*'' making his way down narrow Amsterdam streets and thanking God for legal hashish.

The anxiety in the theater was tangi-

Photographs by ANNIE LEIBOVITZ

Testino the portraitist allows his sitters to 'seem in control of how they look. There is an implied permission. When photographing, he will wait for his subjects to arrive at the moment when they are confident enough to give the [best] version of themselves. It is his ability to reveal the allure that he sees … that has made some of the most photographed people in the world appear as if for the first time in his pictures.' Diana was the woman whom cameras followed everywhere, even to her death. But Testino's are the photos by which we remember her at her most glamorous.

Glamour was also a watchword of *V.F.* mainstay Herb Ritts, a photographer who jump-started his career, quite literally, at a service station. Aged twenty-six, the L.A. native was out for a ride in the desert in 1978 with his friend Richard Gere, an up-and-coming actor, when their car got a flat. As they stopped for a tyre change, Ritts took out his camera and caught a buff Gere, his long locks flowing and a cigarette dangling from his lips. The impulsive, laid-back snaps became publicity stills, helping to etch Gere's smouldering image in the minds of Hollywood casting directors.

Such spontaneity and looseness became a Ritts signature

(figs 40, 41). 'I always found the lack of pomposity in his work, the absence of artifice and pretence, to be a relief', observes Ingrid Sischy, *Interview* editor (and a *V.F.* contributor). 'I liked the fact that most of his portraits are natural, direct … Somehow, he knew how to talk a subject … some of them as high-maintenance as it gets … into a picture in such an easygoing way that there was never blood on the floor.'

Such was the case on a 1990 Malibu shoot for *Vanity Fair* with his friend Julia Roberts. As the actress was slipping out of one of her dresses for the photo session, Ritts noticed she was wearing a pair of Jockey shorts. Ritts later recounted, 'I said, "Those are great." She goes, "Oh, those are my boyfriend's." I said, "Let's just do shorts." … There was not one person on the beach. The water had to be 45, 50 degrees. She threw on a T-shirt, and we ran down to the water. She was down there before I was. I couldn't get the camera out of the case fast enough. She dove under and popped out, and then she just screamed, and it was like therapy almost … this was a total release – and it was her!' (Another gleeful Ritts shot of Roberts appears on p.171.)

Over time, Ritts became Hollywood's fresh prince of

glamour, often rendering the top stars of film and music as gentle giants. And his personality shimmered in every take. Most of his best frames, with their straightforward composition, brimmed with his own openness, daring and boundless optimism. 'He loved shooting at five o'clock', says Harris. 'Always at sunset, often on the beach. The stuff was sexy, without being too tacky. It was pre-digital, so it was warm, natural light, like photojournalism.

'He didn't editorialize', Harris asserts. 'He got that old Hollywood glamour thing in the most genuine way. He captured that kind of "temple of the gods" quality, larger than life. It was heightened realism that looked natural but was better than real, often with a fair amount of retouching, which is what old Hollywood photography was about.'

'He was the most beloved photographer', remembers Susan White. 'Herb's subjects fell in love with him and became his friends. He was their neighbour, in their community, a local. He wasn't a predator, and because of that his subjects had a relaxed demeanour and seemed at ease. His shoots always had a "We're all in it together" feel. You could feel his warmth in their faces. The picture

a photographer takes is as much about the photographer as it is about the subject.'

Definitive Instants

Similar energy, authenticity and edge characterize the work of Harry Benson, Mary Ellen Mark, Jonathan Becker, Helmut Newton and Bruce Weber.

As a portraitist with a photojournalist's acumen, Benson has no peer. He possesses a knack for capturing the powerful, the photographically averse and the hitherto unseen in their inner sanctums (such as New York mayor Ed Koch in his bedroom, p.154). A blessedly restless Scotsman, Benson received his early training on London's Fleet Street and in conflict zones (from Cyprus to the civil rights movement, from the West Bank to Northern Ireland), developing a preternatural radar for gauging the rhythms of a breaking-news picture story so as to move in on a subject at a definitive instant.

'Harry started as a news photographer, a raw group of critters to spring from', the producer/director James L. Brooks has observed. 'He has refused to stray for too long from his roots, even though those roots appear

38

Fig.38
Steamfitter by Lewis Hine, 1920

Fig.39
'Martina Navratilova' by
Annie Leibovitz
Vanity Fair, December 1994

truly grungy alongside the top assignments from high-gloss magazines that constantly roll in like silk from the worm farm. [Some of his pictures require] an extraordinary, pardon me please, set of balls, which is also a consistent element in Harry's life and work.'

'You cannot ever forget he's in the room,' says White, 'not for one second. If all you have is ten minutes, I would trust Harry to come away with the shot almost more than anybody in the world. At the end of the day, he's a photojournalist delivering a story. He wants reality. There are no fluffers – no hair and make-up. The current fashion in portraiture is more an imagined moment. Harry wants the actual moment. He doesn't want to fake it. Sometimes, though, it gets a little too real.'

'Harry has a point of view', adds Harris. 'His photographs say, "You can never take it all too seriously. It's a wonderful life." That's refreshing and reassuring. There's an excitement – radiantly upbeat – to his pictures. When he shoots, he does Cartier-Bresson's "decisive moment", capturing the present that just passed.'

In her own way, Mary Ellen Mark also depicts her subjects with a mesmerizing vérité. Though she has made probing images of

well-known figures for *Vanity Fair* (director Tim Burton, writer Paul Bowles, entertainer Liza Minnelli [p.184]), she is a humanistic photojournalist at heart, her best work quite literally rescuing ordinary and often disenfranchised people from oblivion. As such, she has, like Benson, become that rare hybrid: a master documentarian *and* portraitist.

So too Jonathan Becker, who used his photojournalist's wiles to make his sensitive but devastating rendering of photographer Robert Mapplethorpe, diminished by disease, in a wheelchair and surrounded by admirers (p.161). At other times, Becker casts his special burnished, golden light on members of high society, giving their rarefied spheres a lost-world enchantment.

Having trained at the side of the great Brassaï, and inherited his Rolleiflex from consummate society photographer Slim Aarons, Becker has become the chronicler of aristocrats and aristotrash, grandes dames and Bright Young Things. Equal parts documentarian, anthropologist and artist to the court of the highborn and -bred, he sometimes arrives at cocktail hour, when the light turns to honey, and charms his subjects with wit, canny insight and empathetic banter. 'Jonathan is the world

he photographs', White insists. 'He's a bon vivant with access to socialites. He's inside and he's outside. He really sees a moment worth photographing because his frame of reference is sophisticated, urban, social. And yet he's making a statement about that person with a discerning eye. He's devilish in the details…'

'His best work is in "the enclave", the world of the privileged – warts and all', says Harris. 'Women on staircases and in doorways. They're respectful images, but judgement is being passed. Those two qualities make up the best of what he does – with a touch of Brassaï and Helmut Newton creepiness.'

Which brings us to Newton, around whom the bitten apples of portraiture, luscious or gleaming or rotten, have perpetually fallen.

Helmut Newton's haunting images can be seen as dreamscapes, his attempts at re-envisioning the fears and fantasies of his youth: the backstreets of nocturnal Berlin, the scenes he glimpsed on the city's subways (where he lugged his first camera at the age of twelve), his vagabond, kaleidoscopic existence as he fled Hitler's Germany at eighteen, landing in Australia via Singapore, then on to England and France, where in time he would hijack

Martina Navratilova

Nowhere is the penalty for not facing
reality harsher than on Centre Court at Wimbledon.
A true champion can rise above a
messy pulmeny suit, but when the legs are gone and
the breath is short, the whole world sees it.
Martina Navratilova left at the right time, in the right
way, losing only in the finals—to an opponent
who was one year old when
Martina played her first Wimbledon.
Way to go.

fashion photography with his
erotic obsessions. Newton left
the day's subtler hours to other
photographers; he favoured
the harshness of noon or midnight's
sheen. He preferred cool over
hot, artificial over natural, power
over pity. In his pioneering fashion
photographs, he was forever
ennobling female sexuality,
even if at times he was branded
a misogynist.

In his portraits, Newton was a
master of the stark, extreme close-
up, photojournalistic in its frankness.
He liked to place his camera in
an obeisant position, shooting
upward to inflate his subject's
scale and stature in relation to
the viewer. Among his favourites
was a 1991 study of Margaret
Thatcher (p.169), which he printed
at a commanding six and a half
by four feet for the National
Portrait Gallery, London. In the
portrait, her piercing eyes, perfect
coif and tight-lipped expression
project assurance and authority.
According to renowned collector
Leon Constantiner, who began
acquiring photographs after an
initial encounter with a series of
Newton prints, 'Helmut told me
she was the sexiest woman in the
world because she represented
power and she was the [world's]
most powerful' at the time he
photographed her.

Newton's *Vanity Fair* portraits
of powerful men (Germany's
chancellor Helmut Kohl against a
tree; financier Evelyn de Rothschild
holding a gold bar in the family's
London bank vault; Fiat's honorary
chairman, Gianni Agnelli, in
leonine profile, p.168) were shot
from low angles as well. 'Helmut
was attracted to the dangerous
underside of any person or
situation', White recalls. 'He
wanted the craven, the criminal.
To him, no one was benign.
I called him up once and asked
him to do a certain society figure.
"She's disgusting", he said. "I'd
love to photograph her." He said
it with such relish.' Harris has also
observed that 'Even in his portraits
of businessmen, he found this
dark subtext of subversion,
fetishism and sexuality. I think he
owns that entirely. There's almost
a theatrical sense that comes
from his youth.'

In an era of motor drives and
second takes, Newton exposed
relatively modest amounts of film
on a given assignment. 'Such
stealth and thrift and intensity',
Harris remembers. 'He once
shot six shots, total, of a French
or Italian actress, whom he
photographed topless. When the
film arrived, on the same roll he
had another six frames of another
woman, completely nude, whom

none of us knew. It was probably
a waitress back at his hotel to
whom he had said, "You have nice
breasts. May I photograph you?"'

Newton always seemed to be
in search of the fleeting, seductive
Now. 'In his entire opus,'
Karl Lagerfeld once remarked,
'there is not the slightest trace
of nostalgia.' By comparison,
Bruce Weber shoots fluid
scenes – perfectly imagined and
romance-tinged – that have
irretrievably slipped away. 'Bruce's
photography is all about longing,'
Harris believes, 'longing for a past
youth, a love that never was, an
idealized family.'

Weber, a onetime theatre and
film student who, in the 1960s,
was influenced by photographer
Lisette Model, went on to create
ad campaigns for Calvin Klein,
Ralph Lauren, Abercrombie & Fitch
and others that infused the fashion
world with a fresh yet eroticized all-
American buoyancy. 'Each picture
is reportage-y, a story about a
situation', says White. 'They don't
feel posed, but they are posed.
They're clean and sexy – not
innocent, but intrigued by youth.

'What Bruce has done is idealize
a certain aspect of American
life. He captures a nostalgic,
wholesome optimism, which is
one way we like to see ourselves.
His photos are aspirational. They

create desire – for an object, a
lifestyle, even a sense of self. This
manufactured yearning had a
pivotal impact: he perfected the
lifestyle photograph in the eyes of
advertisers, and their ads haven't
looked the same since.'

Weber, though well-known for
photographing ebullient youth
(such as actor Matt Damon, p.194),
is also masterful when it comes
to bestowing dignity upon those
of advanced years. Weber, like
the poet Walt Whitman, considers
every living thing significant,
from the youngest child to the
slenderest blade of grass. 'He's
the great humanist', Harris says.
'He'll shoot the president of the
United States and the
superintendent of your building
and give them the same nobility.'

Vanity Fair's chief editors have
treated their photographers
(not to mention their writers and
illustrators) as Whitman might
have done, valuing them for their
individual visions, their points of
view and their ability to examine
the world and say, Behold.

Ninety-Five Years of Icon Crafting

Vanity Fair's portraiture tends
toward the polished and theatrical
as opposed to the unvarnished

Fig.42
'Double Exposure', photograph
by Jonas Karlsson
Vanity Fair, January 2004

Ambassador Joseph Wilson and
his wife, CIA agent Valerie Plame,
agreed to pose in front of the
White House at the height of the
storm over the leak of her identity
as an undercover operative.
The photo exclusive received
substantial media attention.

Fig.40
Barbra Streisand, *Vanity Fair* cover
by Herb Ritts, September 1991

Fig.41
Brad Pitt, *Vanity Fair* cover by
Herb Ritts, December 2001

and informal. The magazine, after all, is part of a publishing company that has thrived by valuing quality, recognizing excellence, heralding those who help change the culture and promoting the trappings of achievement and the good life, high style and the arts. As such, V.F.'s photographic tone over the years, despite its often ironic, antic, or decadent content, has been generally glossy and stylized. That style has been characterized by pin-sharp focus, compositional symmetry, elaborate productions in lush settings and sometimes impossibly perfect lighting. The images retain a formality for all their flair.

Unlike portraits in most other magazines, which seem to have been taken by a generic eye, V.F.'s have the imprint of a recognizable *auteur*. Here Jonas Karlsson's ingenuity and transfixing amber glow, Mark Seliger's playful spirit, Nigel Parry's coolness and austerity, Michael O'Neill's crisp concision, the effortless elegance of Timothy Greenfield-Sanders. There the unbridled Technicolor camp of David LaChapelle, the winning levity of Peggy Sirota and Firooz Zahedi, the *noir* nightscapes of Larry Fink, the architectural fidelity of Todd Eberle, whose images, Harris notes, 'are so perfect you could lay a T square onto them'.

As a rule, the magazine has avoided many of the photographic fads of the past three decades. There has been little cross-processing or flash-blur haloing or purely digital confabulation. No serial decapitations, tilt-frame horizons, street-style faux-documentary work. There has been hardly a hint of 'heroin chic' chicanery – no runny eyeliner or carefully mismatched attire in dank rumpus rooms. There are neither hyper-real computerized scenes of oversaturated hue nor large-scale dioramas with emotion-neutral subjects suspended in a stasis of washed-out colour.

That said, *Vanity Fair* has covered much of the rest of the waterfront, from glamour to masquerade to portraiture-as-grand-performance, from jarringly clinical close-ups (novelist Norman Mailer by Irving Penn, p.138; bad-boy author Martin Amis by Nigel Parry, p.167) to environmental portraits (architect Richard Meier by Horst P. Horst, p.175; designer Florence Knoll Bassett by Todd Eberle, p.215), to large-format *mise-en-scènes* borrowing the conventions of film stills (George Clooney as an epic, Fritz Lang-style director, by Leibovitz, p.221) and an astute selection of archival imagery, courtesy of the magazine's peerless photo-

research team. In the process, readers have come to expect that when they open each issue they will receive their requisite ration of visual octane.

Vanity Fair's portraits are also distinctive for their unparalleled access (Becker in Buckingham Palace with Prince Charles and Camilla Parker Bowles; Benson in the hallowed halls of Eton) and for the sheer audacity of the photographers' powers of persuasion (Leibovitz coaxing a topless Miles Davis into bed – with his trumpet, p.152; Karlsson getting CIA agent Valerie Plame – her identity masked by a Grace Kelly headscarf and sunglasses – to pose with her ex-ambassador husband, Joseph Wilson, in a convertible in front of the very White House from which Bush-administration officials had launched a venomous whisper campaign against them [fig.42]).

Since no portrait can reveal a person's authentic depth – only the photographer's interpretation, or the viewer's bias, or the sitter's attempt to project an imagined self – portraiture acts as a form of visual shorthand in the age of runaway fame, a period in which the Internet and 24-7 news foster the impulse to make snap judgements and end up blurring the boundaries between public

Former ambassador Joseph C. Wilson and his wife, C.I.A. operative Valerie Plame, are at the center of controversy over President Bush's bogus claim, in last year's State of the Union address, that Saddam had tried to buy uranium in Africa. The Justice Department is investigating who leaked Plame's covert status—a federal crime—to columnist Robert Novak, presumably as payback for her husband's public suggestion that the White House's intelligence was false. VICKY WARD gives an intimate portrait of the couple that the administration has tried to "slime" in order to "defend" Bush's Iraq policy

I SPY
Joseph Wilson and his wife, Valerie Plame, in Washington, D.C., on November 8, 2003. When they met at a reception, in February 1997, it was love at first sight. "She did not let anyone into the conversation, and I did not let anyone into the conversation," he says.

DOUBLE E XPOSURE

PHOTOGRAPH BY JONAS KARLSSON

and private, formal and vernacular, art and commerce, exhibitionism and voyeurism, appearance and substance, image and identity. Each magazine portrait touches in some way upon one or more of these ambiguities.

Vanity Fair's modern-era photographers, in the end, have taken on the mantle of their Jazz Age counterparts, who helped perfect a new genre: the personality portrait. They have proved themselves worthy heirs to Edward Steichen, who was, in the words of photography scholar Joel Smith, 'the founding *auteur* of a century of celebrity'.

The result has been that image-making, in the pages of *Vanity Fair*, is at times a triumph of icon crafting. Countless Polaroids and pixels have been sacrificed in the creation of a single persona-defining portrait. In short, *Vanity Fair*, in the judgement of the editors of *American Photo*, is nothing less than 'the ground zero of modern iconography', an indispensable gauge for defining who matters in the culture – and how distinctively they inhabit their public image in our media-steeped age.

Sources
See also Select Bibliography, p.246.

Slim Aarons, *A Wonderful Time: An Intimate Portrait of the Good Life*, New York: Harper & Row, 1974.

Anonymous, 'Annie Leibovitz', in *American Photo*, March/April 2000, p.46.

——, 'Bruce Weber, Getty Images, Lifetime Achievement Award, 2005', The International Center of Photography 2005 Infinity Awards.

Harry Benson, *People: Photos/Harry Benson*, San Francisco: Chronicle Books, 1991.

——, *First Families*, Boston: Bulfinch Press, 1997.

——, *Harry Benson: Fifty Years in Pictures*, New York: Abrams, 2001.

Susan Bright, *Art Photography Now*, New York: Aperture, 2006.

Philip Brookman, *Arnold Newman*, New York: Taschen, 2000.

Tina Brown, 'Editor's Letter', *Vanity Fair*, September 1992, p.8.

David Carr, 'A Painted Lady of Magazines, with Gravitas', *The New York Times*, p. 20 March 2006, sec. C.

——, 'Citizen Bono Brings Africa to Idle Rich', *The New York Times*, 5 March 2007.

Graydon Carter, 'Editor's Letter', *Vanity Fair*, November 1992, p.14.

——, 'Editor's Letter', *Vanity Fair*, February 2002, p.38.

Frank Crowninshield, 'In Vanity Fair', *Vanity Fair*, October 1914.

Maureen Dowd, 'Liberties; Feathered and Tarred', *The New York Times*, 10 June 1998.

Jeffrey Elbies, 'The 100 Most Important People in Photography', *American Photo*, May-June 2005, p.63.

Geraldine Fabrikant, 'At Vanity Fair, Successor Finds His Footing', *The New York Times*, 9 September 1996, D1.

Henry Fairlie, 'The Vanity of "Vanity Fair"', *The New Republic*, 21 March 1983, p.25.

Carol Felsenthal, *Citizen Newhouse*, New York: Seven Stories Press, 1998.

David Friend, 'Shooting Past 80', *Vanity Fair*, January 2001, p.112.

——, 'Masters of Photography: Edward Steichen', *Vanity Fair*, September 2003, p.354.

Neal Gabler, *Life: The Movie: How Entertainment Conquered Reality*, New York: Vintage, 2000.

Nan Goldin, *I'll Be Your Mirror*, New York: Whitney Museum/Scalo, 1996.

Lisa Granatstein, 'Eminence Graydon', *Mediaweek*, 10 March 2003, SR10.

Manfred Heiting, *Helmut Newton: Work*, New York: Taschen, 2001.

Julie V. Iovine, 'An Architect Finds Her Buzz', *The New York Times*, 14 November 2002.

Annie Leibovitz, *Photographs: Annie Leibovitz, 1970–1990*, New York: Harper Collins, 1992.

——, *A Photographer's Life, 1990–2005*, New York: Random House, 2006.

Barbara Leibovitz, dir., *American Masters*, 'Annie Leibovitz: Life Through a Lens', PBS, 2007.

Thomas Maier, *Newhouse*, New York: St Martin's Press, 1994.

Tom Mathews, 'High Gloss News', *Newsweek*, 1 May 1989, p.54.

Cathleen McGuigan, 'Annie Leibovitz's Amazing "Life in Pictures"', *Newsweek*, 2 October 2006.

Helmut Newton, *Big Nudes*, London: Schirmer/Mosel, 2004.

Bree Nordenson, 'Vanity Fire', *Columbia Journalism Review*, January/February 2007.

Frank Rich, 'The "Seinfeld" Hoax', *The New York Times*, 13 May 1998.

Herb Ritts, *Notorious*, Boston: Bulfinch Press, 1992.

Hal Rubenstein, 'Demi No Dummy', *Interview*, July 1996, p.88.

Phil Silvers (lyrics) and James Van Heusen (music), 'Nancy (With the Laughing Face)', Milwaukee: Hal Leonard Publishing, 1944.

Ingrid Sischy, 'Masters of Photography: Herb Ritts', *Vanity Fair*, March 2007, p.361.

Joel Smith, *Edward Steichen: The Early Years*, Princeton, N.J.: Princeton University Press, 1999.

Mario Testino, *Any Objections?*, New York: Phaidon, 1999.

——, *Mario Testino Portraits*, Boston: Bulfinch Press, 2002.

Erica Werner, 'Photographer Herb Ritts Dead at Age 50', *Toronto Star* (*via Associated Press*), 27 December 2002.

James Wolcott, 'The First 500', *Vanity Fair*, September 2002, p.302.

VANITY FAIR PORTRAITS 1983-2008
THE PLATES

Norman Mailer, New York
by Irving Penn 1984

David Hockney
by Helmut Newton 1975 (published in *Vanity Fair* Prototype 1982)

Claus von Bülow
by Helmut Newton 1985

Raquel Welch
by Bill King 1984

Jennifer Lopez
by Firooz Zahedi 1998

Jessica Lange and Sam Shepard
by Bruce Weber 1984

Drew Barrymore
by George Hurrell 1984

Arthur Miller and Inge Morath
by Jonathan Becker 1991

Miles Davis
by Annie Leibovitz 1989

Mariel Hemingway
by Annie Leibovitz 1983

Mayor Edward Koch
by Harry Benson 1989

President and Mrs Ronald Reagan
by Harry Benson 1985

Helen Mirren
by Snowdon 1995

The Miller Sisters
L-R: Pia Getty, Princess Alexandra von Fürstenberg, Princess Marie-Chantal of Greece
by David Seidner 1995

Lord Glenconner and attendants
by Lichfield 1985

Princess Caroline of Monaco with her children
L-R: Andrea Albert Pierre Casiraghi, Charlotte Marie Pomeline Casiraghi, Pierre Rainier Stefano Casiraghi, Princess Caroline
by Karl Lagerfeld 1988

Robert Mapplethorpe and admirers
by Jonathan Becker 1988

Daryl Hannah
by Steven Meisel 1989

Jessye Norman
by Annie Leibovitz 1988

Seamus Heaney
by David Barry 1991

Gianni Agnelli
by Helmut Newton 1997

Margaret Thatcher
by Helmut Newton 1991

Sylvester Stallone and Brigitte Nielsen
by Herb Ritts 1985

Philip Johnson
by Josef Astor 1996

Philip Glass
by Chuck Close 2001

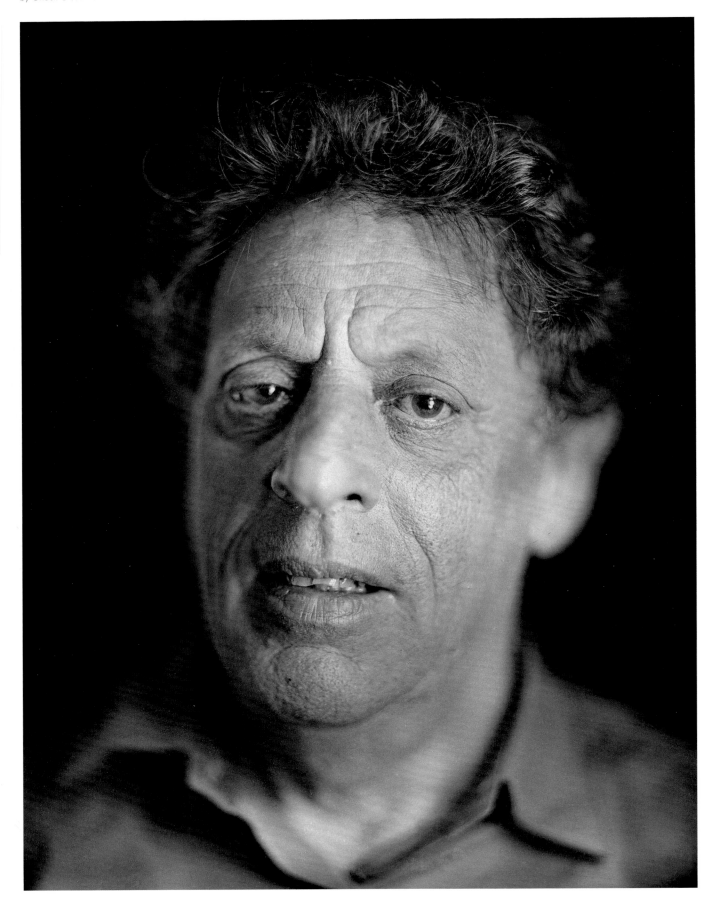

Radiohead
L-R: Colin Greenwood, Ed O'Brien, Thom Yorke (not pictured, Jonny Greenwood and Phil Selway)
by Julian Broad 2000

Diana, Princess of Wales
by Mario Testino 1997

Prince William of Wales
by Mario Testino 2003

Liza Minnelli
by Mary Ellen Mark 2001

Jack Nicholson
by Annie Leibovitz 1992

Arnold Schwarzenegger
by Annie Leibovitz 1997

Shakespeare & Co.
L–R: Greg Vinkler, William Houston, Harriet Walter, Sir Ian McKellen, Rupert Evans, Dame Judi Dench, Morven Christie, F. Murray Abraham, Patrick Stewart, Claire Lautier, Chuk Iwuji
by Mark Seliger 2006

Directorial Titans
L-R: Martin Scorsese, Steven Spielberg, Francis Ford Coppola, George Lucas
by Annie Leibovitz 1996

The Redgraves
L-R: Natasha Richardson, Rachel Kempson, Daisy Bevan, Vanessa Redgrave, Joely Richardson
by Annie Leibovitz 1998

Nicole Kidman
by Annie Leibovitz 1997

Gisele Bündchen
by Walter Chin 1999

Sean Connery and Michael Caine
by Michael O'Neill 1998

Legends of Hollywood
L–R: Nicole Kidman, Catherine Deneuve, Meryl Streep, Gwyneth Paltrow, Cate Blanchett, Kate Winslet, Vanessa Redgrave, Chloë Sevigny, Sophia Loren, Penélope Cruz
by Annie Leibovitz 2001

Boris A. Berezovsky
by Harry Benson 1997

Lance Armstrong
by Annie Leibovitz 1999

Julianne Moore
by Michael Thompson 2000

Filmmakers on the set of *Shaft Returns*
L-R: Samuel L. Jackson, Richard Roundtree, Gordon Parks, John Singleton
by Norman Jean Roy 2000

Rupert Murdoch
by Annie Leibovitz 1994

President George W. Bush and his War Council
L-R: Secretary of State Colin Powell, Vice President Dick Cheney, President Bush, National Security Advisor Condoleezza Rice,
White House Chief of Staff Andrew Card, CIA Director George Tenet, Secretary of Defence Donald Rumsfeld
by Annie Leibovitz 2001

Firefighters near Ground Zero, Manhattan (Men of Engine Company 50, Ladder Company 19)
by Jonas Karlsson 2001

Sofia Coppola
by Annie Leibovitz 2003

John Currin
by Todd Eberle 1999

Florence Knoll Bassett
by Todd Eberle 2003

George Clooney at Universal Studios
by Annie Leibovitz 2005

Tom Cruise, Katie Holmes and Suri Cruise
by Annie Leibovitz 2006

Natalia Vodianova
by Patrick Demarchelier 2004

Hilary Swank
by Norman Jean Roy 2004

Scarlett Johansson and Keira Knightley
by Annie Leibovitz 2005

THE LIGHTS MUST NEVER
GO OUT, THE MUSIC MUST
ALWAYS PLAY.

W. H. AUDEN, 1939

LIST OF LENDERS

Lenders are listed in alphabetical order, followed by the relevant page numbers.

All photographs are Courtesy Condé Nast unless otherwise stated.

Courtesy of the Artist: 152, 153, 164, 165, 179, 186, 190, 191, 198, 208, 209, 210, 212, 213, 221, 223, 228

Courtesy of the Artist & Gagosian Gallery: 214, 215

Courtesy of the Artist and Pace MacGill / Courtesy of Adamson Editions, Washington DC: 176

Josef Astor: 174

David Barry: 166

Collection Timothy Baum, New York: 65

Courtesy of Jonathan Becker: 148, 161

Photograph courtesy of Harry Benson: 154, 155, 200

Collection of Lisa Berman, New York: 202

Julian Broad: 177

Brown Brothers, Sterling, PA: 43

The Cecil Beaton Studio Archive at Sotheby's: 114

Walter Chin: 195

Michel Comte / I-Management: 181

George Eastman House: 57, 66, 76, 94, 96, 103

The Helmut Newton Estate / Maconochie Photography: 140, 141, 149, 168

Courtesy Herb Ritts Foundation: 163, 171, 172, 173

Courtesy Howard Greenberg Gallery: 101

International Center of Photography, David Seidner Archive: 157

Courtesy Jerome Robbins Dance Division, The New York Public Library for the Performing Arts, Astor, Lenox and Tilden Foundations: 40

Dafydd Jones: 201

Jonas Karlsson: 210

Karl Lagerfeld: 159

Lichfield Studios Limited: 158

Collection of Kathryn MacLeod, New York: 187, 203

Mary Ellen Mark: 184

Steven Meisel Studio: 162

Courtesy of Michael Shapiro Photographs, San Francisco: 75

National Portrait Gallery, London: 47, 48, 54, 67, 151, 169, 182

National Portrait Gallery, Smithsonian Institution: 104

Michael O'Neill: 196

Nigel Parry / CPI: 167

Private Collection: 143

Private Collection, New York: 81

Private Collection, UK: 61

The Robert Mapplethorpe Foundation: 160

Norman Jean Roy: 206, 227

Collection of Howard Russeck: 68

Promised gift of Prentice and Paul Sack to the Prentice and Paul Sack Photographic Trust of the San Francisco Museum of Modern Art: 78

Collection of Jane Sarkin, New York: 192

Mark Seliger: 188

Michael Senft, East Hampton, New York: 71

Lord Snowdon: 156

Courtesy of Staley-Wise Gallery, New York: 79

Wendy Stark: 73

Mario Testino: 183, 218, 219

Michael Thompson: 204

Victoria & Albert Museum: 69

Bruce Weber: 144 and 145, 194

Susan White, Director of Photography, *Vanity Fair*: 217

PICTURE CREDITS

Every effort has been made to contact copyright holders; any omissions are inadvertent and will be corrected in future editions if notification is given to the publisher in writing.

The National Portrait Gallery is grateful to *Vanity Fair*, the Condé Nast Archive, and the photographers, owners and copyright holders who have kindly agreed to make their images available to this catalogue.

Essays

Fig.01
'The Return of the Prodigal',
Vanity Fair cover, October 1933

Fig.02
Adolf Hitler, *Vanity Fair* cover by Paolo Garretto 1932
Vanity Fair, November 1932

Fig.03
'9/11', photograph by Adam Woodward 2001
Vanity Fair, September 2002

Fig.04
President Bill Clinton and Vice President Al Gore,
Vanity Fair cover by Annie Leibovitz 1997
Vanity Fair, November 1997

Fig.05
Actor and environmental activist Leonardo DiCaprio
and Knut, a polar bear cub, *Vanity Fair* cover
by Annie Leibovitz 2007
Vanity Fair, May 2007

Fig.06
Mme Pavlova in *Le Cygne, Dress and Vanity Fair* cover
by Schneider of Berlin 1913
Vanity Fair, December 1913

Fig.07
Broadway actor Clifton Webb, comedian Jimmy Savo
as *sommelier* and film star Irene Dunne, *Vanity Fair* cover
by Anton Bruehl July 1934

Fig.08
'Dolores – Personifying the Spirit of Vanity',
by Baron De Meyer 1919
Vanity Fair, December 1919
Courtesy Condé Nast Archive

Fig.09
Lillian Gish, 'Like Pensive Beauty Smiling in Her Tears',
in her role as Lucy Burrows in *Broken Blossoms*, by
Baron De Meyer 1919
Vanity Fair, August 1919
Courtesy Condé Nast Archive

Fig.10
Frank Danby by E.O. Hoppé 1911
Vanity Fair, November 1915
Courtesy Condé Nast Archive

Fig.11
Mary Pickford, 'The Best Known Actress in the World',
by Ira L. Hill 1915
Vanity Fair, October 1915

Fig.12
Douglas Fairbanks, Sr and Mary Pickford
by Nickolas Muray 1922
Vanity Fair, December 1922
Courtesy Condé Nast Archive

Fig.13
'Mary Pickford Grown Up, The Film Favourite Has Finally
Staged a Successful Rebellion Against Little Girl Rôles'
by Edward Steichen 1927
Vanity Fair, September 1928

Fig.14
'Photography Comes into the Kitchen'
by Margaret Watkins 1921
Vanity Fair, October 1921

Fig.15
'Portrait of an American Family: 1924'
by Edward Steichen 1924
Vanity Fair, May 1924

Fig.16
'The White Door' by Charles Sheeler 1917
Vanity Fair, April 1923

Fig.17
Virginia Woolf by Maurice Beck and
Helen MacGregor 1924
British *Vogue*, May 1924 and *Vanity Fair*, September 1929
© Reserved / Private Collection

Fig.18
Virginia Woolf by Maurice Beck and
Helen MacGregor 1924
Variant pose published in *Vanity Fair*, September 1929
© Reserved / Private Collection

Fig.19
Josephine Baker by Paolo Garretto 1935
Vanity Fair, February 1936
© Condé Nast Publications Inc.

Fig.20
Josephine Baker by George Hoyningen-Huene 1929
Vanity Fair, October 1934
© Condé Nast Publications Inc.

Fig.21
Josephine Baker by George Hoyningen-Huene 1931
Vanity Fair, February 1931
© Condé Nast Publications Inc.

Fig.22
George Grosz by Horst P. Horst 1933
Vanity Fair, November 1933

Fig.23
King Fuad of Egypt and German president
Paul von Hindenburg by Dr Erich Salomon 1931
Detail published in *Vanity Fair*, December 1932
Courtesy Condé Nast Archive

Fig.24
Ethel Waters in the Irving Berlin-Moss Hart
musical *As Thousands Cheer*
by Anton Bruehl and Fernand Bourges 1933
Vanity Fair, January 1934
© Condé Nast Publications Inc. / Courtesy
Condé Nast Archive

Fig.25
'Parade of the old-timers at Billy Rose's Music Hall'
by Anton Bruehl and Fernand Bourges 1934
Vanity Fair, December 1934
© Condé Nast Publications Inc. / Courtesy
Condé Nast Archive

Fig.26
Lillian Gish by Edward Steichen 1932
Vanity Fair, December 1932
© Condé Nast Publications Inc.

Fig.27
Marlene Dietrich in *Desire* by Anton Bruehl
and Fernand Bourges 1935
Vanity Fair, January 1936
© Condé Nast Publications Inc.

Fig.28
Vanity Fair cover by Milton Glaser 1983
Vanity Fair, inaugural issue, March 1983

Fig.29
Self-portrait, *Vanity Fair* cover by David Hockney 1975
Vanity Fair, June 1983

Fig.30
Philip Roth, *Vanity Fair* cover by Irving Penn 1983
Vanity Fair, September 1983

Fig.31
Mark Felt, 'I'm the Guy They Called Deep Throat',
photograph by Gasper Tringale 2005
Vanity Fair, July 2005

Fig.32
'The Last Place on Earth', photograph
by Sebastião Salgado 1993
Vanity Fair, July 1993

Fig.33a
Madonna, *Vanity Fair* cover by Herb Ritts 1986
Vanity Fair, December 1986

Fig.33b
Madonna, *Vanity Fair* cover by Helmut Newton 1990
Vanity Fair, April 1990

Fig.33c
Madonna, *Vanity Fair* cover by Steven Meisel 1991
Vanity Fair, April 1991

Fig.33d
Madonna, *Vanity Fair* cover by Steven Meisel 1992
Vanity Fair, October 1992

Fig.33e
Madonna, *Vanity Fair* cover by Mario Testino 1996
Vanity Fair, November 1996

Fig.33f
Madonna, *Vanity Fair* cover by Mario Testino 1998
Vanity Fair, March 1998

Fig.33g
Madonna, with Rupert Everett, *Vanity Fair* cover
by Mario Testino 2000
Vanity Fair, March 2000

Fig.33h
Madonna, *Vanity Fair* cover by Craig McDean 2002
Vanity Fair, October 2002

Fig.33i
Madonna, with Djimon Hounsou, *Vanity Fair* cover
by Annie Leibovitz 2007
Vanity Fair, July 2007

Fig.34
Jennifer Aniston, *Vanity Fair* cover by Mario Testino 2005
Vanity Fair, September 2005

Fig.35
Carolyn Bessette Kennedy, *Vanity Fair* cover
by Bruce Weber 1999
Vanity Fair, September 1999

Fig.36
Cindy Crawford and k. d. lang, *Vanity Fair* cover
by Herb Ritts 1993
Vanity Fair, August 1993

Fig.37
Whoopi Goldberg, 'Making Whoopi', photograph
by Annie Leibovitz 1984
Vanity Fair, July 1984

Fig.38
Steamfitter, by Lewis Hine 1920
Courtesy National Archives and Records Administration,
Records of the Work Projects Administration

Fig.39
'Martina Navratilova', photograph by Annie Leibovitz 1994
Vanity Fair, December 1994

Fig.40
Barbra Streisand, *Vanity Fair* cover by Herb Ritts 1991
Vanity Fair, September 1991

Fig.41
Brad Pitt, *Vanity Fair* cover by Herb Ritts 2001
Vanity Fair, December 2001

Fig.42
Joseph Wilson and Valerie Plame, 'Double Exposure',
photograph by Jonas Karlsson 2003
Vanity Fair, January 2004

Plates 1913-1936

Page 40
Vaslav Nijinsky in *Schéhérazade* by Baron De Meyer 1911
Vanity Fair, May 1916
Courtesy Jerome Robbins Dance Division, The New York
Public Library for the Performing Arts, Astor, Lenox
and Tilden Foundations

Page 41
Anna Pavlova by Eugene Hutchinson 1915
Vanity Fair, September 1920
Courtesy Condé Nast Archive

Page 42
H.G. Wells by Compton Collier 1916
Vanity Fair, June 1916
Courtesy Condé Nast Archive

Page 43
Irving Berlin by Brown Brothers 1914
Vanity Fair, December 1914
© Brown Brothers, Sterling, PA

Page 44
William Orpen by Malcolm Arbuthnot 1916
Vanity Fair, July 1916
Courtesy Condé Nast Archive

Page 45
Augustus John by Malcolm Arbuthnot 1920
Vanity Fair, February 1920
Courtesy Condé Nast Archive

Page 46
Willa Cather by E.O. Hoppé 1921
Vanity Fair, October 1921
Courtesy Condé Nast Archive

Page 47
Thomas Hardy by E.O. Hoppé 1913
Vanity Fair, February 1920
by permission of the E.O. Hoppé Estate Collection /
Curatorial Assistance Inc., Pasadena, California. /
National Portrait Gallery, London (NPG P310)

Page 48
George Arliss by Baron De Meyer 1918
Vanity Fair, June 1919
© National Portrait Gallery, London (NPG P167)

Page 49
Charlie Chaplin by Baron De Meyer 1920
Vanity Fair, January 1921
Courtesy Condé Nast Archive

Page 50
Lillian and Dorothy Gish in D. W. Griffith's *Orphans
of the Storm* by James Abbe 1921
Vanity Fair, November 1921
© Kathryn Abbe / Courtesy Condé Nast Archive

Page 51
Adele Astaire and Fred Astaire by James Abbe 1926
Vanity Fair, September 1927
© Kathryn Abbe / Courtesy Condé Nast Archive

Page 52
Russian Masters by Arnold Genthe 1923
L-R: Ivan Moskvin, Constantin Stanislavski, Feodor
Chaliapin (seated), Vassily Katchaloff, Savely Sorine
Vanity Fair, June 1923
© Condé Nast Publications Inc. / Courtesy
Condé Nast Archive

Page 53
Les Six by Isabey 1921
L-R: Germaine Tailleferre, Francis Poulenc, Arthur
Honegger, Darius Milhaud, Jean Cocteau (sitting
in for Louis Durey), Georges Auric
Vanity Fair, October 1921
Courtesy Condé Nast Archive

Page 54
James Joyce by Berenice Abbott 1926
(unpublished)
© Berenice Abbott / Commerce Graphics Ltd, NYC /
National Portrait Gallery, London (NPG P609)

Page 55
George Bernard Shaw by Malcolm Arbuthnot 1920
Vanity Fair, February 1920
Courtesy Condé Nast Archive

Page 56
Aldous Huxley by Charles Sheeler 1926
Variant pose published in *Vanity Fair*, August 1927
© Condé Nast Publications Inc. / Courtesy
Condé Nast Archive

Page 57
D.H. Lawrence by Nickolas Muray 1924
Vanity Fair, January 1924
© Condé Nast Publications Inc. /
Courtesy George Eastman House

Page 58
Agnes De Mille by Nickolas Muray 1928
Vanity Fair, June 1928
© Condé Nast Publications Inc. / Courtesy
Condé Nast Archive

Page 59
Margaret Severn by Arnold Genthe 1923
Vanity Fair, January 1924
© Condé Nast Publications Inc. /
Courtesy Condé Nast Archive

Page 60
Rebecca West by Maurice Beck and Helen
MacGregor 1924
Vanity Fair, March 1924
© Condé Nast Publications Inc. / Courtesy
Condé Nast Archive

Page 61
Virginia Woolf by Maurice Beck and Helen
MacGregor 1924
Variant pose published in *Vanity Fair*, September 1929
© Reserved / Private Collection

Page 62
The Sitwells by Cecil Beaton 1929
T-B: Sacheverell, Edith, Osbert Sitwell
Vanity Fair, August 1929
© Condé Nast Publications Inc. / Courtesy
Condé Nast Archive

Page 63
Anita Loos by E.F. Foley 1925
Vanity Fair, February 1926
Courtesy Condé Nast Archive

Page 64
Ernest Hemingway by Helen Pierce Breaker 1928
Vanity Fair, September 1928
Courtesy Condé Nast Archive

Page 65
Gertrude Stein by Man Ray 1922
Vanity Fair, August 1922
Courtesy Condé Nast Archive

Page 66
Isadora Duncan at the portal of the Parthenon,
Athens by Edward Steichen 1920
Vanity Fair, June 1923
© Courtesy Joanna T. Steichen / Carousel Research Inc. /
Courtesy George Eastman House

Page 67
Edward Gordon Craig, Notre Dame, Paris
by Edward Steichen 1920
Vanity Fair, August 1924
© Courtesy Joanna T. Steichen / Carousel Research Inc. /
National Portrait Gallery, London (NPG P509)

Page 68
Frida Kahlo and Diego Rivera by Peter A. Juley 1931
Vanity Fair, September 1931
© Condé Nast Publications Inc. / Courtesy Peter A. Juley
& Son Collection, Smithsonian American Art Museum
J0033259

Page 69
Georgia O'Keeffe by Alfred Stieglitz 1918
Vanity Fair, August 1928
© Victoria & Albert Museum / Georgia O'Keeffe Museum

Page 70
Igor Stravinsky by George Hoyningen-Huene 1927
Vanity Fair, November 1927
© Condé Nast Publications Inc. / Courtesy
Condé Nast Archive

Page 71
Pablo Picasso by Man Ray 1932
Vanity Fair, October 1934
© Man Ray Trust / ADAGP, Paris and DACS, London 2007

Page 72
W.C. Fields by Edward Steichen 1925
Vanity Fair, July 1925
© Condé Nast Publications Inc. / Courtesy
Condé Nast Archive

Page 73
Fanny Brice by Edward Steichen 1923
Vanity Fair, June 1923
© Condé Nast Publications Inc. / Courtesy
Condé Nast Archive

Page 74
Léonide Massine in costume for the ballet *Le Carnaval*
by Maurice Beck and Helen MacGregor 1923
Vanity Fair, November 1923
© Condé Nast Publications Inc. / Courtesy
Condé Nast Archive

Page 75 (left)
La Nijinska in make-up for the Larionov ballet *Kikimora*
by Man Ray 1922
Variant pose published in *Vanity Fair*, November 1922
Courtesy of Michael Shapiro Photographs, San Francisco

Page 75 (right)
La Nijinska in make-up for the Larionov ballet *Kikimora*
by Man Ray 1922
Vanity Fair, November 1922
Courtesy Condé Nast Archive

Page 76 and cover (back flap)
Douglas Fairbanks, Jr and Joan Crawford, Santa Monica,
by Nickolas Muray 1929
Vanity Fair, October 1929
© Condé Nast Publications Inc. / Courtesy
Condé Nast Archive

Page 78
Noel Coward, New York by Edward Steichen 1932
Variant pose published in *Vanity Fair*, November 1932
© Condé Nast Publications Inc. / Promised gift of Prentice
and Paul Sack to the Prentice and Paul Sack Photographic
Trust of the San Francisco Museum of Modern Art

Page 79
Josephine Baker by George Hoyningen-Huene 1929
Variant pose published in *Vanity Fair*, October 1934
© Condé Nast Publications Inc. / Courtesy of Staley-Wise
Gallery, New York

Page 80
Amelia Earhart by Max Peter Haas 1933
Vanity Fair, October 1933
Courtesy Condé Nast Archive

Page 81
Leni Riefenstahl by Martin Munkacsi 1931
Vanity Fair, January 1934
© Joan Munkacsi / Courtesy Howard Greenberg Gallery,
New York / Image Courtesy Condé Nast Archive

Page 82
Albertina Rasch Dancers by Florence Vandamm 1927
Vanity Fair, April 1927
© Condé Nast Publications Inc. / Courtesy
Condé Nast Archive

Page 84
Bill 'Bojangles' Robinson by George Hurrell 1935
Vanity Fair, June 1935
© Condé Nast Publications Inc. / Courtesy
Condé Nast Archive

Page 85
Alice White by Florence Vandamm 1928
(unpublished)
© Condé Nast Publications Inc. / Courtesy
Condé Nast Archive

Page 86
Tsuguharu Foujita by André Kertész 1933
Vanity Fair, January 1933
© Condé Nast Publications Inc. / Courtesy
Condé Nast Archive

Page 87
Elsa Jack von Reppert Bismarck by Rolf Mahrenholz 1931
Vanity Fair, October 1931
© Condé Nast Publications Inc. / Courtesy
Condé Nast Archive

Page 88
Jean Cocteau by Cecil Beaton 1934
Vanity Fair, July 1935
© Condé Nast Publications Inc. / Courtesy
Condé Nast Archive

Page 89
George Grosz by Emil Bieber 1928
(unpublished)
Courtesy Condé Nast Archive

Page 108
Colette by Edward Steichen 1935
Vanity Fair, August 1935
© Condé Nast Publications Inc. / Courtesy
Condé Nast Archive

Page 109
Greta Garbo by Edward Steichen 1928
Vanity Fair, October 1929
© Condé Nast Publications Inc. / Courtesy
Condé Nast Archive

Page 110
Babe Ruth by Nickolas Muray c.1930
Vanity Fair, January 1935
© Condé Nast Publications Inc. / Courtesy
Condé Nast Archive

Page 111
Jesse Owens by Lusha Nelson 1935
Vanity Fair, September 1935
© Condé Nast Publications Inc. / Courtesy
Condé Nast Archive

Page 112
Jean Harlow at home by George Hurrell 1934
Vanity Fair, January 1935
© Condé Nast Publications Inc. / Courtesy
Condé Nast Archive

Page 113
Cary Grant by George Hoyningen-Huene 1934
Vanity Fair, November 1934
© Condé Nast Publications Inc. / Courtesy
Condé Nast Archive

Page 114
Katharine Hepburn by Cecil Beaton 1935
Vanity Fair, July 1935
© Condé Nast Publications Inc. / Courtesy
Sotheby's, London

Page 115
Peter Lorre as Raskolnikov in *Crime and Punishment*
by Lusha Nelson 1935
Vanity Fair, January 1936
© Condé Nast Publications Inc. / Courtesy
Condé Nast Archive

Page 116
'Ethel Merman singing "Eadie Was a Lady"'
by Anton Bruehl and Fernand Bourges 1933
Vanity Fair, March 1933
© Condé Nast Publications Inc. / Courtesy
Condé Nast Archive

Page 117
Judith Wood after performing in the show *Dinner at Eight*
by Anton Bruehl and Fernand Bourges 1933
Vanity Fair, April 1933
© Condé Nast Publication Inc. / Courtesy
Condé Nast Archive

Plates 1983–2008

Page 138
Norman Mailer, New York by Irving Penn 1984
Vanity Fair, May 1984
© 1984 Condé Nast Publications Inc. / Courtesy
Condé Nast Archive

Page 139
Susan Sontag, New York by Irving Penn 1983
Vanity Fair, October 1983
© 1983 Condé Nast Publications Inc. / Courtesy
Condé Nast Archive

Page 140
David Hockney, Piscine Royale, Paris
by Helmut Newton 1975
Vanity Fair, Prototype April 1982
© The Helmut Newton Estate / Maconochie Photography

Page 141
Claus von Bülow by Helmut Newton 1985
Vanity Fair, August 1985
© The Helmut Newton Estate / Maconochie Photography

Page 142
Raquel Welch by Bill King 1984
Vanity Fair, October 1984
© Bill King / Collection of Janet King McClelland

Page 143
Jennifer Lopez by Firooz Zahedi 1998
Vanity Fair, July 1998
© Firooz Zahedi

Pages 144 and 145
Jessica Lange and Sam Shepard by Bruce Weber 1984
Vanity Fair, October 1984
© Bruce Weber

Page 146
Drew Barrymore by George Hurrell 1984
Vanity Fair, July 1984
© Estate of George Hurrell, courtesy of George Hurrell Jr /
Image Courtesy Condé Nast Archive

Page 147
Rob Lowe by Nan Goldin 1983
Vanity Fair, February 1984
© Nan Goldin, Courtesy of the Artist

Page 148
Arthur Miller and Inge Morath by Jonathan Becker 1991
Vanity Fair, November 1991
© Jonathan Becker

Page 149
Billy and Audrey Wilder by Helmut Newton 1985
Vanity Fair, November 1985
© The Helmut Newton Estate / Maconochie Photography

Page 151
Jackie and Joan Collins by Annie Leibovitz 1987
Vanity Fair, March 1988
© Annie Leibovitz / Contact Press Images /
Courtesy of the Artist

Page 152
Miles Davis by Annie Leibovitz 1989
Vanity Fair, August 1989
© Annie Leibovitz / Contact Press Images /
Courtesy of the Artist

Page 153
Mariel Hemingway who starred as Dorothy Stratten
in the Bob Fosse film *Star 80* by Annie Leibovitz 1983
Vanity Fair, January 1984
© Annie Leibovitz / Contact Press Images /
Courtesy of the Artist

Page 154
Mayor Edward Koch by Harry Benson 1989
Vanity Fair, April 1989
© Harry Benson, 1989

Page 155
President and Mrs Ronald Reagan by Harry Benson 1985
Vanity Fair, June 1985
© Harry Benson, 1985

Page 156
Helen Mirren by Snowdon 1995
Vanity Fair, November 1995
© Snowdon

Page 157
The Miller Sisters by David Seidner 1995
L-R: Pia Getty, Princess Alexandra von Fürstenberg,
Princess Marie-Chantal of Greece
Vanity Fair, June 1995
© International Center of Photography,
David Seidner Archive

Page 158
Lord Glenconner and attendants, Mustique
by Lichfield 1985
Vanity Fair, January 1986
© Lichfield Studios Limited

Page 159
Princess Caroline of Monaco with her children
by Karl Lagerfeld 1988
L-R: Andrea Albert Pierre Casiraghi, Charlotte Marie
Pomeline Casiraghi, Pierre Rainier Stefano Casiraghi,
Princess Caroline
Vanity Fair, December 1988
© Karl Lagerfeld

Page 160
Ed and Melody by Robert Mapplethorpe 1988
Vanity Fair, February 1989
© The Robert Mapplethorpe Foundation,
Courtesy Art + Commerce

Page 161
Robert Mapplethorpe with admirers at the opening
of his retrospective exhibition at The Whitney Museum
of American Art in New York by Jonathan Becker 1988
Vanity Fair, February 1989
© Jonathan Becker

Page 162
Daryl Hannah by Steven Meisel 1989
Vanity Fair, October 1993
© Steven Meisel / Art + Commerce

Page 163
Kim Basinger, Los Angeles, by Herb Ritts 1989
Vanity Fair, June 1989
© Herb Ritts Foundation

Page 164
Jessye Norman by Annie Leibovitz 1988
Variant pose published in *Vanity Fair*, February 1989
© Annie Leibovitz / Contact Press Images /
Courtesy of the Artist

Page 188
Shakespeare & Co. by Mark Seliger 2006
L-R: Greg Vinkler, William Houston, Harriet Walter,
Sir Ian McKellen, Rupert Evans, Dame Judi Dench,
Morven Christie, F. Murray Abraham, Patrick Stewart,
Claire Lautier, Chuk Iwuji
Vanity Fair, April 2006
© Mark Seliger

Page 190
Directorial Titans by Annie Leibovitz 1996
L-R: Martin Scorsese, Steven Spielberg, Francis Ford
Coppola, George Lucas
Vanity Fair, April 1996
© Annie Leibovitz / Contact Press Images /
Courtesy of the Artist

Page 191
The Redgraves by Annie Leibovitz 1998
L-R: Natasha Richardson, Rachel Kempson, Daisy Bevan,
Vanessa Redgrave, Joely Richardson
Vanity Fair, April 2000
© Annie Leibovitz / Contact Press Images /
Courtesy of the Artist

Page 192
Nicole Kidman at Charleston by Annie Leibovitz 1997
Vanity Fair, October 1997
© Annie Leibovitz / Contact Press Images /
Courtesy of the Artist

Page 194
Matt Damon by Bruce Weber 1997
Vanity Fair, October 1997
© Bruce Weber

Page 195
Gisele Bündchen by Walter Chin 1999
Vanity Fair, January 2000
© Walter Chin

Page 196
Sean Connery and Michael Caine
by Michael O'Neill 1998
Vanity Fair, April 1999
© Michael O'Neill

Page 198
Legends of Hollywood by Annie Leibovitz 2001
L-R: Nicole Kidman, Catherine Deneuve, Meryl Streep,
Gwyneth Paltrow, Cate Blanchett, Kate Winslet, Vanessa
Redgrave, Chloë Sevigny, Sophia Loren, Penélope Cruz
Vanity Fair, April 2001
© Annie Leibovitz / Contact Press Images /
Courtesy of the Artist

Page 200
Boris A. Berezovsky by Harry Benson 1997
Vanity Fair, November 1997
© Harry Benson, 1997

Page 201
Mick Jagger, Madonna and Tony Curtis
by Dafydd Jones 1997
Variant pose published in *Vanity Fair*, June 1997
© Dafydd Jones

Page 202
Lance Armstrong by Annie Leibovitz 1999
Vanity Fair, December 1999
© Annie Leibovitz / Contact Press Images /
Courtesy of the Artist

Page 203
Kate Winslet in homage to her role in *Titanic*
by Annie Leibovitz 1998
Vanity Fair, April 1998
© Annie Leibovitz / Contact Press Images /
Courtesy of the Artist

Page 204
Julianne Moore as Ingres's 'Grand Odalisque',
New York City, by Michael Thompson 2000
Vanity Fair, April 2000
© 2000 Michael Thompson

Page 206
Filmmakers on the set of *Shaft Returns*
L-R: Samuel L. Jackson, Richard Roundtree, Gordon Parks,
John Singleton by Norman Jean Roy 2000
Variant pose published in *Vanity Fair*, April 2000
© Norman Jean Roy

Page 208
Rupert Murdoch by Annie Leibovitz 1994
Vanity Fair, October 1994
© Annie Leibovitz / Contact Press Images /
Courtesy of the Artist

Page 209
President George W. Bush and his War Council
by Annie Leibovitz 2001
L-R: Secretary of State Colin Powell, Vice President
Dick Cheney, President Bush, National Security Advisor
Condoleezza Rice, White House Chief of Staff Andrew
Card, CIA Director George Tenet, Secretary of Defence
Donald Rumsfeld
Vanity Fair, February 2002
© Annie Leibovitz / Contact Press Images /
Courtesy of the Artist

Page 210
Firefighters near Ground Zero, Manhattan
(Men of Engine Company 50, Ladder
Company 19) by Jonas Karlsson 2001
Vanity Fair, November 2001
© Jonas Karlsson

Page 212
Sofia Coppola by Annie Leibovitz 2003
Vanity Fair, December 2003
© Annie Leibovitz / Contact Press Images /
Courtesy of the Artist

Page 213
Robert De Niro by Annie Leibovitz 2000
Vanity Fair, April 2000
© Annie Leibovitz / Contact Press Images /
Courtesy of the Artist

Page 214
John Currin by Todd Eberle 1999
Vanity Fair, February 2000
© Todd Eberle

Page 215
Florence Knoll Bassett by Todd Eberle 2003
Vanity Fair, January 2004
© Todd Eberle

Page 217
Run DMC by Jonas Karlsson 2005
L-R: The Reverend Joseph 'Run' Simmons
and Darryl 'DMC' McDaniels
Vanity Fair, November 2005
© Jonas Karlsson

Page 218 and back cover
Madonna by Mario Testino 1996
Vanity Fair, November 1996
© Mario Testino

Page 219
Jennifer Aniston by Mario Testino 2005
Vanity Fair, March 2006
© Mario Testino

Page 221
George Clooney at Universal Studios
by Annie Leibovitz 2005
Vanity Fair, March 2006
© Annie Leibovitz / Contact Press Images /
Courtesy of the Artist

Page 223
Tom Cruise, Katie Holmes and Suri Cruise
by Annie Leibovitz 2006
Vanity Fair, October 2006
© Annie Leibovitz / Contact Press Images /
Courtesy of the Artist

Page 224
Natalia Vodianova by Patrick Demarchelier
2004
Vanity Fair, January 2005
© Condé Nast Publications Inc. / Courtesy
Condé Nast Archive

Page 227
Hilary Swank by Norman Jean Roy 2004
Vanity Fair, March 2005
© Norman Jean Roy

Page 228 and cover (front flap)
Scarlett Johansson and Keira Knightley
by Annie Leibovitz 2005
Variant pose published in *Vanity Fair*,
March 2006
© Annie Leibovitz / Contact Press Images /
Courtesy of the Artist

SELECT BIBLIOGRAPHY

See also Sources, pp.37, 135, for additional references.

General

Cleveland Amory and Frederic Bradlee, *Vanity Fair: A Cavalcade of the 1920s and 1930s*, New York: Viking Press, 1960.

Graydon Carter, David Friend and Christopher Hitchens, *Vanity Fair's Hollywood*, New York: Viking Studios, 2000.

Graydon Carter and David Friend, *Oscar Night: 75 Years of Hollywood Parties, From the Editors of Vanity Fair*, New York: Knopf, 2004.

George H. Douglas, *The Smart Magazines*, Hamden, Conn.: Archon, 1991.

David Fahey and Linda Rich, *Masters of Starlight: Photographers in Hollywood*, New York: Ballantine, 1988.

Paul Gallico and Nickolas Muray, *The Revealing Eye: Personalities of the 1920's*, Kingsport, Tenn.: Kingsport, 1967.

Geoffrey T. Hellman, 'Last of the Species, I', *The New Yorker*, 19 September 1942, pp.22–33.

——, 'Last of the Species, II', *The New Yorker*, 26 September 1942, pp.24–31.

——, 'That Was New York: Crowninshield', *The New Yorker*, 14 February 1948, pp.74–81.

Horst, *Salute to the Thirties*, foreword by Janet Flanner, photographs by Horst and George Hoyningen-Huene, notes on plates by Valentine Lawford, New York: Viking Press, 1971.

Michelle Fyne-Lee Kung, 'Vivid Interpretations: The Emergence of Modernism through Celebrity Portraiture in Vanity Fair, 1913–1936', Thesis, Cambridge, Mass.: Harvard College, 2003.

Roy T. Matthews and Peter Mellini, *In Vanity Fair*, London: Scolar Press, 1982.

Wendy Wick Reaves, *Celebrity Caricature in America*, Washington D.C.: Smithsonian Institution, 1998.

Diana Edkins Richardson, ed., *Vanity Fair: Portraits of an Age, 1914–1936*, New York: Clarkson Potter, 1982.

Caroline Seebohm, *The Man Who Was Vogue*, New York: Viking Press, 1982.

Herbert Turner, 'Artemus Ward and "Vanity Fair"', *Vanity Fair*, December 1919, p.63.

James Wolcott, 'Cover Story: The First 500', *Vanity Fair*, September 2002, pp.302–16.

Individual photographers

Harry Benson
Harry Benson, *People Photographs*, San Francisco: Chronicle Books, 1991 (first published in Edinburgh: Mainstream Publishing Company Ltd, 1990).

Anton Bruehl
Bonnie Yochelson, *Anton Bruehl*, New York: Howard Greenberg Gallery, 1998.

Francis Brugière
James Enyeart, *Brugière: His Photographs and His Life*, New York: Knopf, 1977.

Imogen Cunningham
Imogen Cunningham Photographs, with an introduction by Margery Mann, Seattle and London: University of Washington Press, 1970.

Arnold Genthe
Arnold Genthe, *As I Remember*, with 112 photographic illustrations by the author, London, Bombay, Sydney: George C. Harrap & Co, 1937.

David Hockney
David Hockney, *Photographs*, London: Petersburg Press, 1982.

George Hoyningen-Huene
William A. Ewing, *The Photographic Art of Hoyningen-Huene*, London and New York: Thames and Hudson, 1986.

George Hurrell
Mark A. Viera, *Hurrell's Hollywood Portraits – The Chapman Collection*, New York: Harry N. Abrams, 1997.

André Kertész
Nicolas Ducrot, ed., *André Kertész, Sixty Years of Photography*, London: Thames and Hudson, 1972.

David LaChapelle
David LaChapelle, *LaChapelle Land: Photographs*, New York: Simon and Schuster, 1996.

Annie Leibovitz
Mark Holbourn, ed., *Annie Leibovitz: A Photographer's Life 1990–2005*, text based on conversations with Sharon Delano, New York: Random House, 2006.

Annie Leibovitz, *Photographs: Annie Leibovitz 1970–1990*, International Center of Photography, New York in association with the National Portrait Gallery, Washington D.C., New York: HarperCollins, 1991.

Patrick Lichfield
Charles Mosley, *Lichfield In Retrospect*, London: Weidenfeld & Nicolson, 1988.

Man Ray
Timothy Baum, *Man Ray's Paris Portraits: 1921–39*, exh. cat., Washington: Middendorf Gallery, 1989.

Man Ray, *Photographs*, with 347 duotone plates, introduction by Jean-Hubert Martin, London: Thames and Hudson, 1982.

Robert Mapplethorpe
Patricia Morrisoe, *Mapplethorpe, A Biography*, New York: Random House, 1995.

Baron De Meyer
Anne Ehrenkranz, Willis Hartshorn and John Szarkowski, *A Singular Elegance: The Photographs of Baron Adolph De Meyer*, San Francisco: Chronicle, 1994.

Helmut Newton
Helmut Newton, *Helmut Newton Portraits: Photographs from Europe and America*, London: Quartet Books, 1987.

Irving Penn
Merry A. Foresta and William F. Stapp, *Irving Penn: Master Images: The Collections of the National Museum of American Art at the National Portrait Gallery*, Washington, D.C.: Smithsonian Institute Press, 1990.

Herb Ritts
Trevor Fairbrother, *Herb Ritts: Work*, with writings by Richard Martin, Steven Meisel and Ingrid Sischy, in association with the Museum of Fine Arts, Boston, New York: Little, Brown / Bullfinch, 1996.

Erich Saloman
Erich Saloman, *Portrait of an Age*, New York and London: Collier Macmillan, 1975.

David Seidner
David Seidner, *Portraits*, with text by Richard Martin, New York and Paris: Assouline Publishing, 2000.

Charles Sheeler
Theodore E. Stebbins, Jr, and Norman Keyes, Jr, *Charles Sheeler: The Photographs*, Boston: Little, Brown, 1987.

Snowdon
Photographs by Snowdon – A Retrospective, exh. cat., with contributions from Drusilla Beyfus, Simon Callow, Georgina Howell, Patrick Kinmonth, Anthony Powell, Carl Toms and Marjorie Wallace, London: National Portrait Gallery, 2000.

Edward Steichen
Todd Brandow and William A. Ewing, *Edward Steichen: Lives in Photography*, London and New York: Thames and Hudson, 2007.

David Friend, 'Masters of Photography: Edward Steichen', *Vanity Fair*, September 2003, pp.354–70.

Penelope Niven, *Steichen: A Biography*, New York: Clarkson Potter, 1997.

Alfred Stieglitz
Susan Greenough, *The Alfred Steiglitz Collection of Photographs* (two vols. 1886–1922, 1923–37), in association with the National Gallery of Art, Washington D.C., New York: Harry N. Abrams Inc., 2002.

Mario Testino
Patrick Kinmonth, *Mario Testino Portraits*, with contributions from Charles Saumarez-Smith and Alexandra Shulman, London: National Portrait Gallery, 2002.

INDEX

Figures in *italics* refer to captions.

ACKNOWLEDGEMENTS

The National Portrait Gallery and *Vanity Fair* would like to extend special thanks to the publishing teams on both sides of the Atlantic: Claudia Bloch, Robert Carr-Archer, Denny Hemming, Celia Joicey, Ruth Müller-Wirth, Terence Pepper and Andrew Ross in London and Gretchen Fenston, Jessica Flint, David Friend, Betsy Horan, Martha Hurley, Dana Kravis, Leigh Montville, Mimi Park and Shawn Waldron in New York.

In addition, thanks are due to Rob King and Robert Millington of Altaimage Ltd, London; Roberto Conti and the Conti team in Calenzano, Italy; Prudence Cuming Associates Ltd, London (Fine Art Photography); Eric Himmel, New York; Joanna Silver at Herbert Smith LLP, London; Kate Prentice and Andrew Wylie at The Wylie Agency, New York; Alison Effeny; Anne Horton, New York; Vicki Robinson; Michael Schwartz, San Francisco; Catherine Bromley, Susanna Brown, Nicola Burton, Denise Dean, Andrea Easey, Shirley Ellis, Denise Ellitson, Clare Freestone, Sumi Ghose, Michelle Greaves, Magda Keaney, Jonathan Rowbotham, Liz Smith, Pallavi Vadhia and Claire Zammit at the National Portrait Gallery; Dori Amarito, Dina Amarito-Deshan, John Banta, Laura Bell, John Branch, Marianne Butler, Carrie Carlisle, James Cholakis, Pat Craven, Annabel Davidson, Peter Devine, David Fenner, Scott Ferguson, Florence Fletcher, Claire Fortune, Chris Garrett, Chris George, Laura Griffin, David Harris, Annie Holcroft, Claire Howorth, H. Scott Jolley, Joel Katz, Jonathan Kelly, Ellen Kiell, Edward Klaris, Beth Kseniak, Robert Levine, Anjali Lewis, Mary Lyn Maiscott, Sara Marks, Amanda Meigher, Christopher Momenee, Robert Morrow, Adam Nadler, Stephen Nix, Brenda Oliveri, Walter Owen, Henry Porter, Kate Reardon, Elizabeth Saltzman, Sylvia Topp, Steve Walkowiak and Susan White at *Vanity Fair*.